A THEORY OF PRICE CONTROL

A Theory of
Price Control

JOHN KENNETH GALBRAITH
Professor of Economics, Harvard University

HARVARD UNIVERSITY PRESS · CAMBRIDGE · 1952

Library of Congress Catalog Card Number 52–5028

Printed in the United States of America

Foreword

This book originated in two essays, "Reflections on Price Control" * and "The Disequilibrium System," † which I published not long after the end of World War II. In the optimism of the day I regarded them as having no foreseeable practical importance; I wrote them with a view to giving a theoretical interpretation to the wartime experience with price control with which I had been associated. I was led to do so partly, I think, by the example of another, more distinguished Harvard economist who had also, in his time, been charged with the formidable responsibility of fixing prices. Following his service as a member of the Price-Fixing Committee in World War I, Professor F. W. Taussig summarized his reflections on his task in a famous paper "Price-Fixing as Seen by a Price Fixer," ** which for the next fifteen years his graduate students were required to read and ponder. It undoubtedly occurred to me that I should place myself in a position to wreak similar pain on students.

For two or three years the essays were accorded the neglect which, the reasons for its loss considered, I can only wish might have been permanent. Within the last twelve months, however, first the prospect and then the fact of renewed price control have brought me a flood of requests for copies, for permissions to reprint, and of suggestions that they be reprinted. One especially urgent (or flattering) friend even offered to poll a sample of economists on the question of reprinting them in the belief that the response would be persuasive. On yielding to this amiable

* *Quarterly Journal of Economics*, August 1946.
† *The American Economic Review*, June 1947.
** *Quarterly Journal of Economics*, February 1919.

pressure, my first thought was to publish the essays and one more recent one * as they were written without change. Unfortunately for this laborsaving expedient, they contained a considerable amount of comment of purely contemporary interest which needed to be edited out. On a few matters, also, I had changed my mind. Most important of all, there was a great deal more that I wanted to say. In the end I virtually wrote a new book, which, however, as the reader should bear in mind, draws heavily on these essays. Also, what I say depends for its groundwork of experience on World War II. I have not been associated, in any important way, with recent stabilization policy.

I have called this book *A Theory of Price Control* with some slight misgiving. It is with the generalizations concerning price control — price control per se and in the context of full and limited mobilization of resources — that I am concerned. This is by far the greatest lacuna in the economic literature of price control. Much has been written on the history of such controls — indeed, past experiments in price-fixing seem admirably designed to absorb the energies of one kind of economic historian, and in recent times much has also been said on the techniques of price control. There has been very little theoretical interpretation of such control, perhaps partly because the major current of economic thought, at least until recently, has been disposed to deny that it can be of any use, and partly because men have hesitated to invest time in an instrument which, unlike taxes or the rate of interest, could be supposed to have only exceptional and transitory relevance.

Because so little has been written on the theory of controls, I have hesitated over a title which might seem to imply that I was here offering a complete theoretical interpretation of their use. On the contrary, in light of the comparative novelty of the topic, this book can hardly be supposed to be more than a beginning on such

---

* "The Strategy of Direct Control in Economic Mobilization," *Review of Economics and Statistics*, February 1951.

a task. A great deal more could be said. And if real peace continues to elude us and the economies of the United States and other countries of the West remain under tension, the theory of control is fated to become one of the expanding universes of economics.

J. K. G.

Newfane, Vermont
July 20, 1951

Contents

A THEORY OF PRICE CONTROL

CHAPTER ONE

The Prewar View of Price Control

As an important instrument of economic policy, the modern use of direct control of prices and wages can reasonably be said to date only from the early years of the Second World War. No one doubts that efforts by central authority to fix prices and compensation are exceedingly ancient — but little less ancient, perhaps, than the exchange of goods itself. In World War I, moreover, the governments of the leading belligerents engaged in a considerable amount of price- and wage-fixing. But a world of difference separates these earlier efforts from what was done in World War II. What had previously been an expedient designed to meet a particular situation, and one that more often than not was confined in its application to a particular commodity or service, became in the Second World War a comprehensive policy. Controls over prices and wages were the rule; freedom from such regulation was the exception. In such comprehensive form, price and wage control was invoked by all of the major participants with the practical exception of China. In the United States, the United Kingdom, Canada, Australia, and Germany, the control over prices and labor incomes was all but complete. In all these countries, also, there was a formidable organization for the administration of controls. And in all of them such control came to be viewed not only as a central part of the task of inflation control but as integral to the larger strategy of resource mobilization.

This was, in many ways, a remarkable development, for as the twin problems of economic stabilization and resource mobilization for war were viewed by most economists prior to the outbreak of hostilities, no very important role would have been assigned to such measures. On the contrary, to the extent that one is permitted to venture a consensus of his professional colleagues, economists would have deplored any major reliance on price and wage controls. The reasons, assuming that ideological and libertarian preferences on such matters had yielded to the *force majeure* of war, were two, both impressively simple: first, it was believed that such action was unwise and, second, that it was impossible.

II

The belief that general control of prices and wages was unwise derived partly from the absence of any clear indication of the good it would do and more from a considerable certainty regarding the damage that it would cause. The purpose of control was to prevent a general and continuing increase in prices and wages. Such a continuing revaluation of goods and factors, unrelated to changes in output, is inflation. The cause of such an increase in money values, in the simplest and most straightforward view of the matter, was an aggregate of demand in excess of the supply of goods and services currently available to meet that demand. To fix wages and prices, especially perhaps prices, would leave uncorrected and undisturbed the excess of demand that initiated the upward movement. It would merely perpetuate the disparity between demand and supply that the upward movement in values was in the process of eliminating. It was difficult to see that anything useful would be accomplished by the operation.

It was not difficult to see the damage that might result. Freely moving prices, as the first textbook lessons tell, are the rationing and allocating machinery of the economy. They keep demand for goods equal to what is available; they guide resources from less to more important uses. Obviously if prices are fixed they can no longer perform these functions. Assuming these functions to be important — and, prima facie, they are not only important but vital — then the economy must suffer from their being rendered suddenly and arbitrarily inoperative. A technically critical piece of machinery is removed from the economy; it is not evident that anything takes its place. At a minimum, the effect must be some malfunctioning of the economy; at a maximum, it might be chaos.

In addition to the objections to controls on grounds of unwisdom, there was, as I have noted, the further objection on grounds of impossibility. This had exceedingly impressive empirical support. For centuries individuals and economic groups had sought the assistance of political authority to ameliorate by public regulation the inconvenience or oppression of too high or too low prices or too high or too low wages. Even when allowance is made for the lack of sympathy with which such experiments have normally been interpreted by historians, the record still appears to be one of unrelieved botchery and failure. Prior to World War II there did not exist in economic history, so far as I am aware, an important experiment in the public regulation of prices or wages which, in the consensus of its interpreters, was thought to be a brilliant success or even a success. This, as man's efforts at social experiment go, was surely quite a remarkable record of frustration and failure.

There were reasons of apparently impeccable theoretical validity to explain these failures. As just noted, prices and wages rise in response to a demand that is in excess of supply valued at the previous prices. The given supply can be sold at higher prices — it can be sold because buyers, however unhappily, would prefer to pay the higher price than to accept their alternative opportunity which is to do without. The sellers, it can readily be assumed, prefer the higher price to the lower one. Thus, if the price increase is arrested by authority, the action runs not only against the interest of sellers, but also against the interest of those buyers who are not able to satisfy all or substantially all of their wants at the fixed price. An incentive thus exists for a coalition on behalf of higher prices between sellers and at least some buyers. This coalition is based on an equally rational interpretation of immediate self-interest on both sides of the market. The larger the disparity between the fixed and the equilibrium price of the particular commodity or service — the greater its price elasticity of demand — the greater the proportion of all buyers who will be potential members of the coalition. Price-fixing by authority, then, is clearly a case of government without the consent of the governed.

Given the considerable difficulty of policing the prices at which transactions occur, it is more than logical to expect that, at some point, the price-fixing authority will surrender to the coalition against it. In everyday language, a small black market, reflecting the prices which sellers can get and some buyers are willing to pay rather than do without, will become a larger black market, and eventually it will become the only market. And this, perhaps, would not be a bad thumbnail summary of the fate of price-fixing efforts for a thousand years prior to World War II. It is scarcely surprising that price control *qua* price control had no prominent place in the economist's armory of stabilization weapons and that, on the contrary, it was regarded as illusory and self-defeating, a bait for the untutored and the naive.

III

It is part of man's pride that he makes economic policy; in fact, in economic affairs, he normally adjusts his actions, within a comparatively narrow range of choice, to circumstances. This was admirably illustrated by the course of price control policy in World War II. In the end, as I have suggested, all of the highly organized belligerents emerged with comprehensive systems of price-fixing. Yet in no one can the adoption of such controls be said to have been the result of careful policy deliberation and choice. The action appears to have been taken in all cases because, at the moment, circumstances appeared to offer no other course.

The pioneer action, the German price-stop of 1936, was taken by men who were intellectually incapable of weighing the alternatives and who knew only that the German people had a mortal fear of inflation. They proclaimed a ban on price increases because, to their unsubtle minds, it seemed the only way to prevent inflation and was a fine authoritarian gesture to boot. The United Kingdom, not uncharacteristically, backed into a patchwork system of price control and maintained throughout the war what amounted to a voluntary system of wage control by consent of those controlled. The Canadian price ceiling imposed in the autumn of 1941 appears to have been a Cabinet response to a current upsurge in prices. It seems not to have had the approval of those who, at the time, were responsible for what had been a policy of limited price control, and these men were very soon superseded.

In the United States the action was even more clearly dictated by events. During 1941 a broad and markedly orthodox design for wartime price policy had been worked out by those associated with the enterprise. Taxation, supplemented by control of consumer credit and perhaps also of business borrowing, was expected to hold aggregate demand roughly in balance with the supply of goods and services currently available. Within this context, price controls would be applied to commodities which the war had placed in especially short supply or especially strong demand. Control in these markets would, in the normal case, be reinforced by rationing or allocation. By so limiting demand, the special or market equilibrium would be maintained for the particular product.* The question of wage control was elided mostly

---

* This, without any explicit emphasis on rationing, summarizes the policy recommended by Leon Henderson to the House Banking and Currency Committee in 1941 during hearings on what became the Emergency Price Control Act of 1942. Earlier in 1941, in a paper that had appreciable influence on policy design, I had outlined a stabilization strategy along roughly the above lines (*Review of Economic Statistics*, May 1941).

Certainly the most widely read and quite possibly the most influential prescription for wartime stabilization was that of Keynes. He summarized what is, in

for political reasons but partly out of a belief that the regulation of this factor price was peculiarly authoritarian and partly out of the hope that wage stability would be a by-product of price stability.

In the winter of 1942, when the Emergency Price Control Act of that year became law, price control was still being viewed as a measure for dealing with particular equilibrium situations although, by then, the number of situations in which the need for control was foreseen had been greatly — indeed indefinitely — increased. At this point, events rapidly took command. Prices began rising at a rate which, to a public and to public servants not yet inured to real inflationary movements, seemed inordinately rapid. The long debate over price control legislation had served to identify price stability with price control. The passage of the legislation had transferred responsibility for price stability from the Congress to the Executive and within the Executive to those who had sponsored the legislation. The legal procedures that had been developed within the Office of Price Administration for selective price-fixing contemplated carefully considered regulations on each commodity and these procedures were not easily redesigned to make possible more rapid case-by-case action. And even prompt steps to fix many individual prices promised to be too time-consuming and too difficult of equitable administration.

Meanwhile, there seemed to be no immediate prospect of the tax or other fiscal measures that would be sufficient to bring aggregate demand into balance with supply. In any case, some who were then in positions of responsibility were beginning to wonder, as more have since wondered, if wartime price stability, achieved

---

essentials, a similar policy as follows: "It has been argued here that the only way to escape inflation is to withdraw from the market, either by taxation or by deferment, an adequate proportion of consumer's purchasing power, so there is no longer an irresistible force impelling prices upward." He added that "some measure of rationing and price control should play a part in our general scheme and might be a valuable *adjunct* to our *main* proposal" (italics added) [*How to Pay for the War* (London, 1940), p. 51].

through tax and other fiscal measures, was not a rainbow that might be chased indefinitely. Some action to fix all prices legally within reach of control seemed to be the only remaining course of action. The result was the General Maximum Price Regulation. This regulation, promulgated in the spring of 1942, was by all odds the most important single step in wartime price policy and the model for the controls imposed in early 1951. It flatly reversed the earlier design for price control policy. It made no pretense to deal with particular disequilibria; it undertook, quite unequivocally, to fix prices *qua* prices. Events had forced the step that economists, in the main current of economic theory, had so long viewed as unwise or impossible, or both.

The economists responsible for this action were not easy in their minds over the way circumstances were forcing them to flout authority. The Emergency Price Control Act required that formal regulations of the Administrator be accompanied by a Statement of Considerations. The Statement accompanying the General Maximum Price Regulation was the most carefully drafted and edited document of the early Office of Price Administration, and it carefully hedged against the eventual failure of the Regulation. At one point the Statement declared: "There can be no effective price control while at the same time there is so large an amount of excess purchasing power." * And again it stated "Without [adequate taxation, savings and wage stabilization] the ceiling would in the long run become *administratively unenforceable and socially harmful*." † These statements were made partly in the hope of stimulating collateral action on taxes and wages, partly as a warning against what was deemed to be excessive reliance on price-fixing, and partly in the tenuous hope that they might, in the event of failure of the regulation, protect the professional reputations of those responsible.

* *The General Maximum Price Regulation*, Bulletin No. 1, April 28, 1942, p. 24.
† *Ibid*. Italics added.

There is ample room for argument over how well price control worked during World War II in the United States. Its denouement in 1946 was not very graceful; it was followed by persistent inflationary movement. There are resulting grounds for argument — although I shall argue the contrary — that the controls were at best a temporary expedient and that they deferred rather than prevented price movements which were, in any case, bound to occur. But even if this be conceded, it can hardly be argued that price control led to the kind of debacle that prewar theory would have foretold. During the critical war years prices remained comparatively stable in face of a large and continuing excess of aggregate demand over supply. Moreover this stability was achieved, in considerable measure, as the result of price-fixing *qua* price-fixing. For only part of the period of the war and for only part of the total stock of goods was demand, in particular equilibrium situations, adjusted to supply by rationing or its equivalent.

Governments came during these years to look upon price control as an important instrument of stabilization policy. It survived the war, however scathed, with sufficient reputation for effectiveness to insure that, in like circumstances in the future, it would again be invoked. The earlier weight of theory to the contrary, it had been proven possible to perpetuate, at least for a period of years, a disequilibrium at legislated prices.

In the next two chapters the reasons for the unexpected workability of price control *qua* price control in the modern economy are examined. The three chapters following take up its role in the more or less fully mobilized economy and its aftermath. This is price control in that adaptation of the price system to the requirements of wartime planning which was used in World War II and which I have termed the "Disequilibrium System." The final chapters deal with price and wage controls, under conditions of partial mobilization and in relation, therefore, to the kind of inflationary tensions we have recently been experiencing.

Throughout these chapters I have, in general, taken stable values — more accurately, a long-run assurance of a given and assured purchasing power of the dollar — as a desideratum. Except where the matter is integral to my argument, I have not paused to make the case for such stability, either in any great detail for its contribution to effective mobilization or for its importance for preserving property rights and economic equities. It is a case that has been made many times, and I have nothing to add to it. I do regard it, however, as a case of profound importance. Inflation, more than depression, I regard as the clear and present economic danger of our times and one that is potentially more destructive of the values and amenities of democratic life.

CHAPTER TWO

Price Control and Market Imperfection

There has never been any doubt, in theory, of the ability of a price control authority to maintain a fixed price in a particular market if the price-fixing is supplemented by rationing. Rationing, if properly administered, has the well-understood effect of limiting demand to what is available at the fixed price and thus establishing a special market equilibrium that is wholly stable.

During World War II in the United States a considerable number of consumer's goods — mainly foods — were rationed, and a very large number of producer's goods and materials were subject, through the allocation of the entire supply to specified uses, to an equivalent control. To the extent that price control proved effective for these products it needs no explanation.

Price control, however, was also applied to, and worked moderately well for, a large number of unrationed commodities. It was moderately effective for primary metals and other industrial materials before or after they were rationed or allocated, for houseroom throughout the war and after, and for scores, even hundreds of other producer's and consumer's goods, ranging from fluid milk to farm machinery parts, where or when there were no formal controls over demand. In light of prewar conclusions concerning what was possible, this does require explanation.

The explanation is a many-sided one. But the unifying core to which all or nearly all of the facets of the explanation are attached is the nature of the modern industrial market. These markets lend themselves to price regulation to a far greater extent than had previously been supposed.

Specifically, demand in the imperfectly or monopolistically competitive market, especially those that are characterized by small numbers, is subject to an informal control by the seller which is frequently the effective equivalent of rationing. The purely competitive market lends itself to no such control. There is no reason to suppose that the prewar estimate of the workability of price control was greatly in error as applied to the purely competitive market. It erred for the economy as a whole because the susceptibility of the imperfect market to control was not foreseen and the ubiquitous character of these markets was not fully appreciated.

In the purely competitive market, individual buyers and sellers are anonymous; no seller can have a group of buyers who are identified as *his* customers. All buyers and all sellers are fluidly participant in the market. But when the number of buyers is relatively small, or the number of sellers relatively small, or both conditions obtain, the market as an abstract entity disappears. Then sellers and buyers are no longer anonymous; they deal with each other as individuals. It is possible for sellers (or vice versa, the buyers) to allocate scarce supplies to specific customers. If the established price is below the equilibrium price, it is possible and even rather easy for sellers to give large, habitual, or otherwise favored buyers, preference rights to what is available and this is a very natural pattern of behavior. Other sellers do likewise. In the ideal case there is no supply left to enter a free (or black) market; customers having received an appropriate share have a reduced incentive to search for black market supplies. In such markets, in other words, price-fixing is accompanied, *pari passu*, by allocation or rationing. When the government fixes prices, it delegates to sellers in imperfect markets the responsibility of rationing their customers which they, in turn, have the power to undertake. From some points of view this delegation of power and the possibility of its abuse might be disturbing. For present purposes it is sufficient that it can provide an effective control over demand and thus can be an effective buttress for price control.

The efficiency of such private rationing would appear to depend, first, on how sharply customers are identified to the seller. If past purchases of customers are a matter of record, and if the seller knows their needs and the reliability of their claims, he can ration them rather effectively. The identification of buyer with seller becomes increasingly indistinct the more competitors the seller has. There will be an increasing likelihood that customers will have been irregular in their patronage — that they will have shifted between sources of supply and that neither their past purchases nor their normal requirements will be known. With increasing numbers of competitors, moreover, the responsibility which any one seller can assume for fair or otherwise appropriate distribution diminishes. Among other things he becomes progressively less aware of what other sellers are providing and to whom. As a result, some customers, by luck, diligence, or wile, are certain to get more than their appropriate share; others, who for that reason get less, have a powerful motive to bribe some pliable seller into breaking the ceiling. It was commonplace in early OPA experience that the primary metal markets, where sellers are few, were relatively easy to control without formal allocation. The secondary metal markets, with numerous sellers, presented far more difficulties. Even in areas or at times of substantial shortage, control of retail milk prices (almost invariably in a market with few sellers) was effective without formal rationing. Fresh vegetable prices were virtually impossible of such control.

II

The assistance accorded to the price-fixer by the market of small numbers is not exclusively a matter of market rationing. The fact that there are small numbers in the market, combined as this must be in the case of important industries or services with firms of considerable size, is also of notable assistance in the enforcement of price regulations. While it is technically possible for sellers in such imperfect markets to ration their customers at the fixed prices, this is not their most profitable course of action. The more profitable course, the sanctions aside, is to raise prices and break the law. Historically, the consequences of such violation — recalling always that it occurs under circumstances when sellers *can* charge and buyers *will* pay more — has been considerably more disastrous for the price-fixing authority than for those it sought to regulate.

Without doubt, modern price administrators have had a far more law-abiding generation of businessmen with whom to deal than their even less happy predecessors. Also, a community that has come to think of war as a tragedy stigmatizes illegal profiteering as a more heroic age did not. The freebooting contractors who supplied the Continental and Union armies would be appalled by the restraints which public opinion has imposed on their descendants. Moreover, for the first time in World War II, and in greater measure perhaps in the United States than in any other country, price control became a meticulously planned operation.* Price regulations were carefully designed to fit the practices and convenience of individual industries and even of individual firms. This effort to adapt regulation to existing practice rather than to force the adaptation of practice to regulation, greatly aided enforcement.†

---

* I have, however, been reminded that the Edict of Diocletian (301 A.D.) was, in its own way, at least as ambitious. It placed ceilings on something over 900 commodities and 130 or more different types of labor. The latter included such diverse toilers as lawyers, schoolteachers, and bath-house guards. The Edict and its background have been explored in fascinating detail by H. Mitchell, "The Edict of Diocletian," *Canadian Journal of Economics and Political Science*, February 1947, pp. 1–2, recently reprinted in *Outside Readings in Economics* (New York: Crowell, 1951), pp. 460–473.

† This was largely an achievement of the talented legal staff of the Office of Price Administration. It might be added that one consequence was lengthy and elaborate regulations. The apparent complexity of these orders promptly became a target for the type of superficial and irresponsible critic who infests our public

Finally, it was realized from the outset that price control would require active enforcement. In the past, and during World War II in South American countries among others, most price control consisted merely of decrees by remote central governments. There was no machinery for enforcement, and transactions left few of the tracks through banking and accounting systems which complicate the life of the violator in the more highly developed economy. As a result, there was virtual immunity from penalties for violation.

However, enforcement of price control is also much easier in the imperfect than in the more purely competitive market. Where the imperfection is associated with small numbers, the task of policing the controls is obviously simplified by this fact. Much more important, in such markets the initiative to violation must normally be taken by the seller. This deserves a special word.

In the purely competitive market the initiative to violation of a price regulation is, in principle and in all probability in fact, as likely to be assumed by the buyer as by the seller. The buyer is as likely to seek out a seller and offer an illegal premium in order to get the product as the seller is to seek out a buyer and offer to supply him at an illegal price. In the first case and even in appreciable measure in the second case, the buyer is a party to the offense. As such, he is most unlikely to report it.

In the market of small numbers, the initiative to price change normally lies with the seller. Although the price of metal scrap is made by Marshallian bargaining between buyers and sellers, this is not the case with the price of steel. It is set in the first instance by the seller. In the ordinary course of business, the buyer

---

life. He demanded short and simple regulations, but had these been issued he would have attacked them as dislocative and arbitrary, which they necessarily would have been. It is exceptions and qualifications which make such regulations complex but which keep them from being arbitrary.

My imaginative colleague and the subsequent administrator of the OPA, Paul A. Porter, once proposed that I yield to the demands for simplification and fix one price — five dollars, as I recall — for everything.

of steel — the commonplace buyer at least — does not approach the U. S. Steel Corporation to bargain on prices. And he does not do so when steel prices are fixed. Accordingly, if there is to be violation in such markets, the initiative must be taken by the seller. This leaves the buyer detached from the offense and in a position, if he is so disposed, to report it. To generalize more broadly, in the competitive market there is little hope that the buyer will police the price regulations imposed on the sellers; in the imperfect market, the market of administered prices, there is considerable chance that he will.

If market imperfection is associated, as it frequently is, with sellers of large size, there are other reasons why the seller must be circumspect. Illegal action, even if it can be kept off the formal record, must be known to employees including some who will take an impersonal view of their employer's behavior. This involves grave risk of disclosure, and it is a risk of which every large firm is notably wary. The aberrations of a large concern also have more news value than those of a small one, and the large seller also has lawyers to tell him how to obey the law and public relations counselors to advise him to do so.

III

The next major respect in which the imperfect market assists the price-fixer arises from the tendency for prices to be inflexible and also, in some measure, institutionalized, in such markets. Where the seller has control over his prices — and *ex hypothesi* he has some measure of control in every imperfect market — he may for any one of a number of reasons seek to minimize the frequency of price changes. In some instances, market control, the entente between sellers itself, can be maintained only if prices are stable; the understanding may not be sufficiently complete or durable to survive too many ups-and-downs. In other cases, customers, or the Department of Justice, may have become accustomed to stable prices and may be aroused by change. Changes in prices also may be costly either in money or administrative convenience.* Accordingly, profit maximization in an imperfect market may require that prices be kept constant over substantial periods; the price changes that would be required by any attempt to keep profits at a maximum at every point of time would reduce returns over a period of time.

The phenomenon of inflexible prices had been well-observed before the war, † but so far as I am aware (and for good enough reasons) no one had observed that this inflexibilty would facilitate wartime control. The contribution was considerable. Not only had buyers and sellers in markets characterized by rigid prices become accustomed to the level of the price, but they had also become familiar with the differentials, discounts, special deals, and all the other appurtenances of the price structure. It is much easier to continue and enforce such a settled and familiar structure than to check the upward surge of a more nearly competitive market. And in competitive markets, because differentials and discounts, like the level of prices itself, may change in day-to-day bargaining, no price schedule is as likely to conform neatly to a past structure. So, precisely at the time when sellers or market operators in such markets lose the prospect of higher prices or speculative gains, they must alter their business to conform to rules laid down in some not very engaging government prose.

For such sellers, compared with those who have been selling at infrequently changing prices, the discomforts of price control are great. The Office of Price Administration controlled the

---

* For this latter observation and phrase, I am indebted to Robert D. Calkins, who suggests that a surprisingly large number of decisions in both business and government are affected by this cost. He is undoubtedly right.

† Edward S. Mason, 'Price Inflexibility," *Review of Economic Statistics*, May 1938. Gardiner C. Means, *The Structure of the American Economy, Part I*, National Resources Planning Board, June 1939. Donald D. Humphrey, "The Nature and Meaning of Rigid Prices, 1894–1933," *Journal of Political Economy*, October 1937. I venture to refer also to a paper of my own, "Monopoly Power and Price Rigidities," *Quarterly Journal of Economics*, May 1936.

prices of all steel mill products with far less man power and trouble than was required for a far smaller dollar volume of steel scrap. Handlers of farm products complained with especial bitterness of OPA regulations, perhaps partly because it is their nature to complain, but partly because, as participants in competitive markets, their difficulties were greater. I am tempted to frame a theorem that is all too evident in this discussion: it is relatively easy to fix prices that are already fixed.

IV

Infrequent changes in prices may best serve the long-run earnings position of a firm or industry. There is also a strong element of convention in price-making, which works on the side of infrequent change, and which does not directly serve the goal of maximum return. Traditionally (or in textbooks, at least), custom or convention has been considered an exceptional or off-type factor in price-making. The experience of modern wartime price control, I believe, would indicate its more general importance. It, too, helped the price-fixer.

The stronghold of conventional or customary pricing is in distributors' margins, particularly in retail selling. For a large proportion of all retailers and a rather smaller proportion of all retail trade, the price charged for the service is a strictly conventional markup or "mark-on." Sometimes this is the markup suggested by the supplier; sometimes it is conventional with the store or trade for that particular class of merchandise. In either case, price control was invoked in markets in which participants had ceased to look upon price-setting as one of the exploitive or profit-making decisions on which the revenues of the business depended. Accordingly, as shortages developed, it seemed a perfectly normal procedure to the radio dealer, the refrigerator dealer, or even the cigarette vendor, that he sell off his limited stock at his accustomed markup. Quite often he eliminated, sometimes illegally, his accustomed concessions or "markdowns," which he had looked upon as vaguely abnormal. But he did not think of exacting the new and higher markup that the market would have allowed. Had retailers attempted this on any considerable scale, as I, for one, originally supposed they might, OPA enforcement would have been nearly helpless.

The phenomenon of customary or conventional pricing deserves more analysis than it has received. Indeed, the very terms "custom" and "convention" may be deceptive. That many sellers neglect the opportunities for profit maximization in setting prices cannot be doubted. They follow the easy rule of charging what they have charged before or what someone else is charging. Pricing by custom, in this case, represents, no doubt, an atrophy of market motivations; the seller is opting for a habitual rather than a profitable pattern of behavior. But I suspect that what is called custom is more often an indispensable simplification of what otherwise would be an inordinately complex task. The small retailer, and often the larger one, has neither the information nor the capacity to adjust his margins commodity by commodity, week by week, or season by season, in such manner as might maximize his returns. It is of special significance, I think, that retail margins *are* the stronghold of customary pricing. Here the individual seller typically dispenses a large number of items. To arrive at a theoretically right price or margin for each would require that he solve a formidable array of simultaneous equations. He lacks the capacity for any such ideal price policy; its mental, if not its monetary, cost would be exorbitant. So he relies on rule-of-thumb.

The effect of a well-designed system of price control in markets of this kind is merely to continue accepted rules. A violation of price ceilings thus means that the seller is abandoning customary business procedures. It calls for a degree of analysis and imagination in the use of prices that is not called into play in the uncontrolled market. Inertia comes strongly to the support of the price control.

This is an advantage, it will be observed, that is likely to work most strongly on the side of the price-control authority when, as in 1941 and 1942, its orders are issued after a long period of stable or slowly changing price levels. With the prices generally in flux, as they were prior to the imposition of controls in 1951, the role of inertia is undoubtedly much less important.

CHAPTER THREE

Price Control and Market Imperfection (Cont'd)

There remain two further features of the imperfect market which make it susceptible of control. The first of these is in the area of supply-price relationships. Its practical manifestation is a considerable lapse of time between an increase in price in an uncontrolled market and the shortage of goods that ensues if that price increase is arrested.

It is obvious that a price-fixer will not have serious trouble maintaining his ceilings while supply remains sufficient at his fixed price. One clear conclusion from the experience of the Office of Price Administration is that it may remain sufficient for a considerable period. Repeatedly the agency was able to forestall strong upward thrusts in prices and hold these prices, while for several months — sometimes a year or two — supply remained abundant. This period of grace was invaluable. While it lasted, the regulations could be perfected: a simple "freeze" of prices could be translated into a workable price schedule, and staff could be assembled to administer the regulation. Meanwhile, enforcement was not difficult, and prices, of course, were stable.

This experience would suggest, to speak somewhat elliptically, that the supply-demand equilibrium is a loose-jointed concept, and that, in the language of an earlier discussion, it is "indetermi-

20

nate." But some analysis is possible. In disturbed times, the demand function, viewed as an independent variable, is not intimately related to current consumption. In the immediate prewar years and in the early years of World War II, there was much anticipatory buying, far more than in a similar upswing of peacetime activity. Especially after the war began, advance buying was no longer a speculative venture in the ordinary sense. It was expenditure on a form of insurance. Where this buying was in anticipation of price increases, that is, where the buyer sought to avoid higher costs later or hoped to realize on increasing inventory values, price control had a unique remedial value of its own for it eliminated or at least weakened the motive to the buying that was causing the price increases.

Before and during the early months of World War II, it seems probable that both businessmen and consumers, guided by their recollections of World War I, were, in their buying, more concerned with protecting themselves from high prices than from prospective shortages. It was high prices rather than shortages that dominated the recollections of the first war. One might guess, therefore, that price control, as a restraint on anticipatory buying, was more effective in 1940–1942 than it would likely be in the future for there can be little doubt that the dominant recollection of World War II is of absolute shortages of goods. Nonetheless, the price controls imposed in early 1951 appear, in the inevitable combination with other factors, to have had some effect in lessening the pressure of anticipatory demand and in contributing to the marked lessening of inflationary tensions which followed.

I am not sure that the period of grace between control and shortage is peculiar to any class of market. During World War II it was noticeable for commodities — coffee, wheat, sugar, cocoa, and pepper — as well as for industrial goods. Without doubt, however, it is also most markedly a phenomenon of imperfect markets. Where price changes are few and the market imperfection is oligopoly, routine shifts in demand must *ex hypothesi* be accommodated at the going price. The result is some margin of excess capacity. In an inflationary context, the decision to increase prices will usually be taken before the excess capacity has been exhausted by increasing demand. If the increase is forestalled, the industry's reserve capacity will enable it to supply its markets, perhaps for a considerable time. As early as December, 1941, the American Tobacco Company initiated a sizable increase in the price of Lucky Strikes. Presumably, the other major companies would soon have followed suit. The increase was disallowed, and in spite of a steady increase in current consumption, there was no shortage even of individual brands for over two years.

II

Finally, price control during World War II was aided by an unsuspected cost behavior of firms in modern markets under conditions of expanding output.

Many, if not most, of the economists actively associated with price control in the early years of OPA consciously or implicitly assumed that where large increases in production would be required, it would be at increasing cost. Some had in mind the bulk-line cost curves of the First World War (it is significant that the term did not gain currency in World War II) and the presumption of increasing cost implicit in these arrays.* For as large an industrial expansion as occurred, they would have predicted rather general increases in prices or else the widespread use of subsidies and differential prices to compensate for higher (marginal) costs.

In retrospect, except for agriculture, the number of industries

---

* Notably in the arrays in Taussig's "Price-Fixing as Seen by a Price Fixer." While there may have been others, the only industry group with an acute recollection of these bulk-line cost curves that I encountered during my service with the OPA was, appropriately enough, the anthracite producers. Members of the industry informally but urgently recommended adherence to the principle that prices be set to cover (full) costs of the highest-cost *necessary* producer. Taussig notes that the anthracite industry was a rich beneficiary of the bulk-line principle.

that were expanded for war purposes at increasing cost seems small. Certainly, the number of manufacturing industries expanded at increasing cost was extremely small. During the early months of price control, a strenuous effort was made to gain acceptance for the principle of using subsidies to offset higher "marginal" costs in increasing-cost industries. This was successful,* and such subsidies were notably useful in maintaining prices of copper, other non-ferrous metals and a few other commodities. In a miscellany of other situations, the same result was achieved through differential pricing. Nevertheless, the area in which these policies proved appropriate was relatively small, and in the main it was in the extractive industries. The policy was not applied except in very limited measure to manufacturing, and the reason, almost certainly, was that most industrial expansion during the war was at constant or decreasing cost.

In principle, this question of whether wartime expansion is obtained at increasing, constant, or decreasing cost has only a derived relation to the problem of price control. Price increases to cover the cost of high-cost output at the margin are not, in the strict sense, inflationary. They contribute to inflation only to the extent that bulk-line firms have more income to dispose, which, especially if it becomes the target of wage demands, adds to the aggregate of excess demand.

In practice, however, avoidance of these price increases is most important. The community is not likely to discriminate between price increases that are needed to cover the cost of increased output in an increasing cost industry and price increases that are in response to the pull of demand. Any increase is, in some measure, a precedent for others.† In a period of general expansion of output,

---

* Credit for this achievement and for saving the government many millions of expenditure belongs primarily to Professor Donald H. Wallace, now of Princeton University.

† I am inclined to believe, however, that the fear of precedent was exaggerated. In fact, experience suggests that a superficially discriminatory, but fundamentally logical, differentiation in price policy as between firms or industries can be explained to principals and even to the Courts.

a tendency toward constant or diminishing costs is, therefore, notably helpful.*

Decreasing costs may be partly attributed to the methods by which wartime capital expansion was financed. Where, for example, the government supplied plant or equipment through the Defense Plant Corporation, the existing supply of fixed plant ceased to be a factor shaping the supply curve. Provided the factors were supplied at constant cost, only the diseconomies of scale — an increasingly unfavorable combination of management with other factors — could be the cause of increasing costs, even in the short run.

However, decreasing costs also achieve their specific importance as a support to price control in combination with oligopoly. Even where price covers cost by a substantial margin, it is by no means certain, especially in the short-run context of war economics, that supply will be forthcoming. Supplementary negotiation is essential to obtain the supply, that is, to keep supply price in normal relation to cost. Such negotiation is only practical where the number of firms is relatively small. The possibility of assembling the members of an industry for negotiation on prices — negotiation that is based on the costs of the individual firms — may appear to be a small matter, but it is one of great importance.

The inability to supplement price control with negotiation for supply based on the actual cost and profit position of the individual firm explains, in some measure, the relative ineffectiveness of price control for agricultural products. The Department of Agriculture did use propaganda on behalf of increased production with considerable success. And during 1943 proposals for entering contracts with individual farmers for expanded production were seriously debated. But, in general, increased farm pro-

---

* For a large number of military items, initial contract prices were very high. As manufacturers gained experience, both in technique and in costing, prices declined spectacularly. While this phenomenon was also generally helpful to the price-fixer, it represents a secular movement not properly a part of this discussion of cost behavior.

duction was obtained during World War II by assuming that the supply price for the quantity wanted (the "goal") was high. This was communicated, as it had to be, to producers en masse; the price so set bore no relation to marginal costs. While this course of action could be defended on grounds of expediency, it is only fair to add that some of its authors in the Department of Agriculture might have approved it with no justification beyond the fact that it led to higher prices.

III

Some conclusions are now in order. In the imperfect market — in particular, in the market of small numbers — price control *qua* price control is a technically workable instrument of economic policy, at least in the short run. If its employment is justified on other grounds, it cannot be rejected, out of hand, as unfeasible. This conclusion is consistent with the accepted theoretical interpretation of such markets and is supported broadly by experience.

The doubts of economists as to the technical workability of price control prior to World War II proceeded not from an error of analysis but from an error of assumption. Price control was appraised in relation to markets which approximated, however roughly, a condition of pure competition. To the extent that this assumption was faulty, and it undoubtedly was faulty in considerable measure, the workability of price control was underestimated. But it is equally important to recognize that the prewar appraisal, as applied to markets characterized by pure competition or an approximation thereto, was generally accurate. Such markets — markets of many buyers and sellers where for each respectively the demand and supply functions are completely elastic at the going price — do exist. Price control, unsupplemented by further measures to reduce the demand in the particular market, can be applied to such markets only with the greatest difficulty and at best with indifferent and temporary results.

This was well-illustrated by World War II experience. While

price control both then and more recently has been viewed as a homogeneous policy of uniform applicability to the economy, in practice its results have not been uniform. Over the great range of manufactured producers' and consumers' goods, both in World War II and in the recent period, price control has been administered with relatively little public fuss and controversy. There have been relatively few complaints of maldistribution of supplies or of black markets. This, by common observation, is the part of the economy where market imperfection is characteristic. The great problems of price control have been encountered in food and clothing, the part of the economy which, with important exceptions, most closely approaches pure competition. At least two-thirds of the energies of the Office of Price Administration were devoted to these products, and a considerably larger fraction of its failures were in this area. The efforts to hold meat prices, before and after an effective rationing system was in effect, provided an almost classic display of the frustrations of price-fixing *qua* price-fixing in the market of many sellers and buyers.

It follows that in markets approaching pure competition, price control, if it is to be maintained in face of any substantial excess of demand over supply, must be supplemented by formal measures to reduce demand in the particular equilibrium situation. This, normally, means rationing. Thus there are markets where prices can be fixed, in face of a considerable excess of demand over supply, without formal rationing controls. There are some, however, where this cannot be done. One of the central tasks of price administration is to distinguish between the two.

IV

In exploring the reasons why price control has been possible, I am a little uneasy lest I appear to have argued that price control is easy. That is a conclusion which no past participant in the effort is likely to reach; it is one which my own former colleagues in the enterprise would assuredly not forgive. For if a kind Providence simplified part of the task, a stern one made other parts more difficult than anyone could reasonably have expected. Certainly few could have guessed how adept and compelling would be the pressures brought to bear on the price-fixer. As economists have long believed, the desire for money is one of the most viable of human motives. And as students of government have long assumed, the urge to reëlection, in its own sphere, is also potent. The price-fixer must contend with and even appear to thwart both of these aspirations, either individually or in a mighty coalition.

No price-fixer can avoid working damage on the fortunes of individuals — if not in an absolute sense, then at least in relation to opportunity. His task consists in denying men income they have had or could have had. When such effect is wrought by the free market there is no one to blame, or at most, the onus attaches subjectively to grasping middlemen, insatiable unions, or Wall Street. When a price-fixer damages a man's fortune or his hope for one, that individual is left in no doubt as to who is responsible or as to the appropriate object of his dislike.

There are also the administrative problems of price control. These have not even yet been fully appreciated. It is a commonplace that price control requires a sizable organization, although the total paid staff in World War II on price control alone — a few thousand — was smaller than many have imagined. It is not a commonplace that this staff must be trained in a relatively subtle subject matter and have at its command a range of information as varied as the American economy itself. To the requirements of high training and intelligence is the further vital one of high probity and strong sense of purpose. In both World War II and in late 1950 and early 1951, the task of assembling such a staff had to be undertaken while, at the same time, the policy itself was being executed. There have surely been few more demanding tasks of government.

CHAPTER FOUR

The Disequilibrium System

Within the last ten years, price control as an instrument of economic policy has been used in two substantially different contexts. During World War II it was used in conjunction with an extensive mobilization of economic resources for military use. The ostensible and, in large measure, the actual objective to which all others were subordinate was the task of mobilization. More recently, price control has been employed with the primary objective of stabilizing prices. This has been done at a time when the economy was under inflationary pressure as the result of arms expenditure. However, only a comparatively small fraction of the total current resources of the economy has been going into defense use; it has not been seriously claimed that these were making preclusive claims on the economy or that price control was motivated for reasons other than the protection of the civilian economy. It is appropriate and even necessary, therefore, to examine price control separately in each of these two contexts. It by no means follows that the policy appropriate in the one case is appropriate in the other. In Chapter V, price control and the companion controls over wage and other incomes are examined in the context of full or relatively full mobilization. First, however, it is necessary to have a full view of the structure of the mobilized economy in which such controls are employed.

II

During World War II the United States, partly by improvisation, partly by plan, developed a system of mobilizing economic resources that, by the commonly accepted standard of results, proved highly satisfactory. The American system was not unique; in its major contours it resembled that of the other belligerents which were forced to make an abrupt conversion from a largely unplanned to a largely planned utilization of resources. It is my purpose, somewhat in the tradition of market theory, to idealize the system that was so devised and to examine its central features.

The form of wartime organization employed by the United States, and with variations by the other major belligerents with the exception of Russia and China, I have termed the "Disequilibrium System." Under this system the incentives and compulsions of an unplanned economy were supplemented or supplanted by three new forces for determining economic behavior. These were (1) a more or less comprehensive system of direct control over the employment of economic resources, (2) a nearly universal control over prices, and (3) an aggregate of money demand substantially in excess of the available supply of goods and services. Because it was a distinctive and pervasive feature of the system, I have used this disequilibrium of demand and supply to name the system as a whole. To these three determinants might be added a fourth which, although supplementary, represented the area of the greatest wartime failure in the United States. That is the use of an effective system of rationing to reinforce price control in those markets that approximate conditions of pure competition.

I am assuming throughout this and the next chapter that the mobilization objective is to attain maximum resource employment of the greatest possible efficiency, to get a militarily optimal allocation of resources between military and civilian use, and to distribute the former between different kinds of production, and present and future output, in accordance with a given but not static plan. These ends should, if possible, be so served that the way is open for eventual restoration of prewar property rights and status and the normal functional mechanics of the economy. This conservative objective is presumably secondary, if as during the last war, the doctrine of total war is avowed. This doctrine — the doctrine that the *only* objective is victory — was asserted by all of the leading belligerents in the last war although it is doubtful if any, with the possible exception of Russia, could be said to have followed it in economic practice.

III

The role of direct controls over resource use in the system can be quickly indicated. For regulating the use of resources, the available choice is between the incentives and compulsions of the market, and authority. Market incentives are incapable of producing the comprehensive transfers in resource employment that any considerable mobilization requires. An effort by the government to monopolize steel supply by offering high prices would necessarily be defeated by the inelasticity of demand for steel by some private buyers. So with other resources. The response to such market incentives would also be highly uncertain. Sellers in imperfect markets who take a comprehensive view of their position do not seek, as earlier noted, to maximize profits at any given point of time. For this reason they will not willingly accept a government order, even though it is immediately more profitable than any alternative, if it promises to impair their long-run position in the market. The automobile industry, in late 1941 and early 1942, was displaying normal market behavior in preferring manufacture of automobiles to tanks or aircraft, even assuming the latter netted higher immediate returns.

All this holds whether or not there is price control. Although for purely administrative reasons the introduction of a comprehensive system of price control probably precludes the use of market incentives on a large scale, it actually makes possible their use within limits. With price control it becomes possible to create *and maintain* a differential return for favored industries. However, this is a detail. For a full-scale mobilization, the government must specify by order where and how plant, materials, and, if the mobilization is complete, labor resources are to be used.

With this very brief comment, I take leave of the subject of direct control over resource use — of the vast subject of materials allocation, control of the use of manpower, procurement, and so forth. This summary dismissal does not mean that I consider this part of the control structure either unimportant or easy to employ. It is neither. But my concern here is with other aspects of the system.

IV

The comprehensive control of prices and the general excess of demand, the two other determinants of economic behavior that are vital to the disequilibrium system, were both the objects of an important miscalculation before the war. Price control, as I have noted, was widely regarded as unwise and technically unworkable. Since a general excess of demand was what made price control unworkable, such an excess would be eliminated by the movement of prices to a new and higher position of equilibrium. Further increments of demand with given supply would be eliminated by a further succession of such movements, that is, by inflation. Since the technical feasibility of holding prices in face of an excess of demand was not recognized, it was not supposed that the latter could exist. It is not surprising, therefore, that the role of an excess of demand in relation to the functioning of a mobilized economy remained unexamined. In World War II such a surplus of demand played an important role, the significance of which we have only gradually perceived.

The aims of wartime industrial mobilization I have defined as the bringing of all possible resources into efficient use and their planned allotment to military and civilian use and between present and future production. The allocation and reallocation of resources by authority presents no problem in principle, and the practical problem, as the wartime experience showed, though difficult is not insuperable. It is not clear, however, that direct controls are similarly effective for ordering normally unused resources, especially labor, into the market. Yet the mobilization of unused labor power is, perhaps, the most important single requirement for a general increase in national output. Such a mobilization was accomplished in the United States with apparent success and with but limited resort to authority. While one needs to be wary of such comparisons, the experience of the United States seems to have compared not too unfavorably with that of England, which used a combination of authority and incentives, and very favorably with Germany, which relied heavily on authority.[*]

The first contribution of excess demand was to provide a taker for anyone who offered his or her services. Frictional unemployment was eliminated, in effect, by providing a market adjacent to every worker.[†] Excess demand, in other words, established and sustained a nearly universal labor shortage. No one who wanted to work could complain of his or her inability to find a job, and no one who did not want to work could plead inability to find employment as an excuse. Once in the labor market, such

[*] The increase in male (native) German workers between 1939 and 1943 did not exceed the natural rate of increase. The number of women gainfully employed actually declined in the early years of the war, and although it was higher by a few hundred thousand at the end of the war, the proportion of all women in gainful employment did not increase. In the early part of the war, there was still some (Nazi) doctrinal objection to use of women in factory work, but it had been subordinated to expediency by 1943 or 1944, and by then the government was actively trying to get women into industry. Cf. *Effects of Strategic Bombing on the German War Economy* (Washington: U. S. Strategic Bombing Survey, 1945), pp. 29 *et seq.*

[†] This consideration led the CED economists to urge the maintenance of an excess of demand (and price control), in the early reconversion period. Cf. *Jobs and Markets*, Research Study for the Committee for Economic Development (New York: McGraw-Hill, 1946).

labor power, even with the slight controls over manpower that were invoked in the United States, became subject to a measure of direction as to use.

However, what may perhaps be called the passive contribution of excess demand was at least as important. I have reference here to the kind of wage and income policy which is permissible when such an excess of demand is being allowed to develop. Its effect is best seen by contrasting what was possible under the disequilibrium system with what could have been done had it been necessary to keep aggregate demand equal to supply at a given level of prices.

To maintain equilibrium would have required energetic measures to restrain the expansion of incomes. Since *ex hypothesi* prices would be stable, hourly rates would not have been under undue pressure. But other contributions to income would have had to be watched with care. Overtime and doubletime would be dangerous, as would payments (usually at inflated productivity rates) to new arrivals in the labor market, and as would payments under incentive schemes. Yet these inducements to labor power at the margin were of the utmost importance for the expansion of output that occurred during World War II; approximately half of the real increase in gross national product between 1940 and 1944 has been attributed to individuals not normally in the labor market and to the increase in the average work week.* It seems reasonable to argue that much of this increase occurred because the disequilibrium system made it possible to advance the price of marginal labor power with almost complete disregard for fiscal consequences.

It was likewise possible to reward the marginal entrepreneur,

* *America's Needs and Resources* (New York: Twentieth Century Fund, 1947), p. 13. The estimates, admittedly crude, attribute 48 per cent of the real increase from 1940 to 1944 to increased hours and "emergency" workers, 26 per cent to absorption of unemployed, 13 per cent to normal increase in the working force, and the rest to increased productivity. Some of the latter can be attributed to the shift from low- to high-efficiency employment encouraged by high take-home pay.

the inefficient old one or the inexperienced newcomer, with a similar neglect of fiscal effects. The relation of taxes to incentives could also be largely elided. Had taxes during World War II approached the rates necessary for equilibrium at prewar prices, their relation to incentives would certainly have become a matter of substantive, as distinct from verbal, concern.

To refocus the discussion somewhat, excess demand during the war was the counterpart of a buffer of unemployed resources, especially unemployed workers — the buffer that is necessary for price stability in the absence of price control. If markets are uncontrolled, any near approach to full employment of normally employed workers will lead, in a strong market, to price increases followed by wage increases or to wage increases followed by price increases.* In the imperfect market where labor costs are established by collective bargaining, there is no basis either in theory or experience for assuming stability in price and factor costs at full employment. On the contrary, as I shall argue in more detail later, there is every reason to expect a continuing interaction of wages and prices. Under the disequilibrium system by contrast, it was possible to dispense with the buffer of unemployed resources which would have been necessary for equilibrium stability and to substitute, through surplus demand, a positive pressure on resource use. It was a practical way of adapting modern capitalism — a capitalism characterized by oligopoly in product markets and strong unions in factor markets — to the wartime imperative that all possible resources be employed and if possible under approximately stable conditions of prices and costs.

During World War II, and in considerable measure afterward, the fact that an excess of demand was allowed to accumulate behind the control structure was viewed as a weakness in fiscal management. Given better management, it would have been appropriated by taxation or, perhaps, stabilized in the hands of its

* Cf. Paul A. Samuelson, *Econometrica*, July 1946, p. 191.

possessors by forced saving. The present argument runs sharply to the contrary. Viewed in relation to the objective of developing maximum military potential, the accumulation of some volume of excess demand was not undesirable. On the contrary, it contributed to, or made possible, a more effective organization of resources than the apparent alternative. However, it also seems certain that few policies need to be administered with closer attention to the limits and to the context within which they are appropriate. I now turn to the limits within which an excess of demand is desirable.

v

The indulgent Providence that (so far) has protected the United States was especially kind in bringing it to the disequilibrium system with a prior faith in the idea of maintaining equilibrium of aggregate demand and supply at a ruling price. For, to the extent that there was a sense of guilt in allowing demand to exceed supply, there was a motive for keeping the excess of demand as small as possible. That was fortunate, for an excess of demand is advantageous and even tolerable only to a point. The volume of demand in excess of current supply that adds to, or is consistent with, additions to aggregate output, I propose to call the "margin of tolerance." It is of the utmost importance for understanding the disequilibrium system to know what determines this margin of tolerance.

The counterpart of the current excess of aggregate demand is, of course, an equivalent volume of current saving. The explanation of the high actual volume of current savings during the war is complex and in considerable measure conjectural. Without doubt, patriotic compulsions, reinforced by Treasury appeals and community pressure, affected the average propensity to save by individuals whose income was not changed. For those whose income was increasing, a low (marginal) propensity to consume may be assumed. But it would seem clear that the proximate cause of much, if not most, of the increased saving was price control. At a minimum, price control associated a variety of inconveniences with spending money; at a maximum, through shortages, it removed a large number of the accustomed objects of consumption. The normal choice between specific objects of consumption and saving could not be exercised. Individuals and firms who had no intention of saving became involuntary holders of cash or its equivalent. The disequilibrium follows from the circumstance that in the absence of price control and attendant shortages, they would have spent their income for the given supply of goods and in so doing would have established equilibrium at a higher price level.*

For individuals who are exercising a normal choice between saving and consumption, who are equating the marginal utility of money to spend with that of money to save, there is no new problem of incentives. For those who may loosely be termed "involuntary savers," incentives become a matter of first-rate importance. It may be assumed that the marginal utility of money for this group will show a tendency to fall as the proportion of savings to total income increases or, secularly, if a given (high) proportion of saving is continued over a long period. When for either or a combination of these reasons it falls to the point where there is a general withdrawal of marginal labor effort, it may be said that the margin of tolerance in the disequilibrium system has been exhausted.

It seems unlikely that in the United States during World War II any such point was reached or even approached. There was the happy circumstance that within the memory of the present generation, the dollar had not gone through hyperinflation. There was no general expectation of a collapse of values as a

* It was once suggested to me that since this group did hold cash balances, the term "forced equilibrium" would be preferable to "disequilibrium." This I judge to be a matter of taste; I opted for the shorter term and for the notion that "equilibrium" is more meaningful, in this context, as a description of the market relationships that would have obtained in the absence of price control.

result of military defeat. Moreover, throughout the war there was a strong conviction that the current high employment and income was merely an interlude between depressions. This elasticity of expectations, to use Professor Lange's term,* was reinforced by manufacturers who promised a flood of inexpensive and elegantly streamline goods after the war and by the Treasury with its rediscovery of the sovereign virtues of thrift. Perhaps most important of all, consumption after savings was high — for most workers higher than before the war. Had there been a sharp reduction in opportunities for current expenditure, workers might well have revised their attitude toward acquiring and holding dollars, the redundancy of which would be a matter of day-to-day observation.

In any case had the ratio of savings to income become too high at some point, or had a less high ratio continued too long, incentives would have been weakened. An admirable arrangement for, in effect, getting current work in return for a promise of future consumption or security would have disintegrated. Workers, equating the marginal disutility of labor effort with diminishing marginal utility of income for saving, would, in the absence of strong patriotic compulsions, have abandoned overtime and Sunday work, and marginal workers would have withdrawn from the market rather than add to their stock of savings. A good thing would have been overdone.

Its large margin of tolerance must be counted one of the major sinews of American strength in World War II, in interesting contrast with Germany where the margin would appear to have been decidedly thin. Because of the inflation of the mark in the twenties, the accumulation of cash balances was clearly a less attractive alternative to spending for Germans than for Americans. It may be doubted if many Germans supposed, even if they won the war, that Hitler would permit them to enjoy a lush, secure peace. Especially from 1943 on, there was a strong under-

* *Price Flexibility and Employment* (Bloomington: Principia Press, 1944).

current of feeling that Germany would, in fact, lose the war. In the United States the principal (although it will be apparent that I now believe mistaken) reason for restraining the expansion of demand was to protect the price controls. In Germany price and rationing controls were perfectly secure — they even survived combat and the fantastic disorganization that followed — and there was no serious wartime black market. Partly for this reason and partly, perhaps, because they were callous practitioners of financial heterodoxy, the German leaders during the war period seem not to have been greatly worried over the expansion of demand.*

As a result, Germany far exceeded its margin of tolerance. Women, as I have noted, were not attracted by the opportunity of earning money in industry; indeed, during the war some employed women apparently withdrew from the labor force as they became beneficiaries of substitute cash income in the form of servicemen's allowances. There was a recognizable tendency for entrepreneurs, especially from 1943 on, to hold materials or inventory, or to acquire equipment, rather than to produce end-products for sale, the result of which would be an increase in cash balances.

In the years between 1945 and 1948, Germany presented a sharply etched picture of a country that had completely exhausted its margin of tolerance and where, as a result, the disequilibrium system had entered the final stages of disintegration. Price control was still fairly effective in face of an approximately sevenfold expansion in the means of payment as compared with prewar years and a fall in output to between a third and a half of prewar volume. This control was supplemented by a reasonably efficient rationing system, and even through much of this period the black market was still fairly limited. A large part of the

* Earlier, as Burton H. Klein has pointed out, orthodox influences were a good deal stronger. "Germany's Preparation for War: A Re-examination," *American Economic Review*, March 1948.

middle class and many workers had all of the money they could spend without working or could acquire it by a few days' work each week. It was all but inconceivable that anyone would work to acquire marks to save. The unwisdom of exchanging scarce energy for redundant marks, in those years of hunger, involved no subjective balance of psychic gain and disutility at the margin. It presented a simple problem of physiology which most Germans readily solved.

VI

It follows from the foregoing that one of the critical tasks of wartime economic management, perhaps the most critical task, is to exploit but not exhaust the margin of tolerance. In order to maximize the output of non-consumable military end-products and investment, the government must use its opportunity to get these in return for currently unspendable money. It must not go so far with this involuntary saving that it weakens incentives.

Over a longer period, the state faces an equally important task of fiscal craftsmanship in so handling matters that the margin of tolerance, to be exploited in emergency, is kept as great as possible. This consists, above all, in maintaining public confidence that savings in any period will have high future value, either for the purchase of goods or for their contingency value for personal security. As I have suggested, the margin of tolerance during World War II was wide. There was the general expectation of a postwar depression when the purchasing power of such savings would increase, as would also the need for them for personal security. Also, the experience with the savings of World War I was favorable — they were subsequently spendable at prices considerably below wartime levels, and the 1921 depression emphasized their importance for personal security.

As a result of developments following World War II, we shall not be so fortunate again. The inflationary increase in prices during these years will be the basis of expectations for the years following any future crisis, if such a crisis is our misfortune. Nor, in my judgment, was this misfortune inevitable; things were managed badly in these years. In refusing to work gradually away from wartime controls and taxes, we dissipated a vital source of national strength. This might have been forgivable, did the condemnation rest only on the subtleties of economic theory. But the lessons of economic theory here coincide, as indeed they usually do, with the copybook maxims which stress the importance of good faith and integrity.

CHAPTER FIVE

Price Control and the Disequilibrium System

It is now time to return to price control. From what has just been said, it will be evident that in the context of full mobilization, price control, including control of wage and other factor payments, is not simply a device for restraining the increases in prices and incomes that are the outward manifestation of inflation. Rather it is part of a complex piece of apparatus which embraces the whole task of mobilization management and which is integral to the problem of getting hitherto unused resources into use and keeping them there. Viewed in this light, how should price (and factor income) controls be managed?

In the broadest sense, the administration of price controls must have two objectives in view. There remains the first and very simple objective of forestalling the movement of prices to equilibrium at higher (and successively higher) price levels in accordance with the current (excess) demand. But price controls must also be administered with a view to restraining the expansion of demand, which, I have argued, would at some point undermine incentives and destroy the system. This is the more subtle task of the price-fixer: to use his instrument to protect the margin of tolerance in the disequilibrium system.

One formula which would serve both ends would be to allow no price increases whatever. When the General Maximum Price Regulation was issued in the spring of 1942 — I identify the launching of the disequilibrium system in World War II with the issuance of this order — a flat prohibition on price increases was proclaimed and reiterated in the subsequent "hold-the-line" orders of October 1942 and May 1943.* In fact, no such policy was possible. Apart from the important circumstance that many costs were left uncontrolled by the first two orders, it meant that all kinds of accidental and often bizarre cost-price relationships would be perpetuated indefinitely. Some of these might induce an undesirable allocation of resources; more could not be defended in equity before the bar of public or congressional opinion.

Nor was any such formula necessary. It is clear, in retrospect at least, that there can be considerable flexibility in the administration of price control in the disequilibrium system, the amount depending in each case on the derived effects of the price increase. This latter will be different in each of three broad (although not mutually exclusive) categories of good or payments. The three categories may be labeled "Wages and Wage Goods," "Non-Wage Civilian Goods," and "War Goods."

II

The allowable flexibility is least in the case of wages and wage goods. Although individual adjustments are not precluded, the disequilibrium system requires that these be firmly anchored. A general advance in wage rates, even though absorbed out of profits, will use up part of the margin of tolerance, if, as may reasonably be assumed, the marginal propensity to consume from wage income substantially exceeds that from profit income. Or, more likely, such an advance will force a general readjustment of prices which, if repeated at intervals, will have a similar effect to

* I am reasonably certain that few, if any, of the economists associated with price control believed such a formula to be workable. Prior to the issuance of the General Maximum Price Regulation, there was, however, deep concern lest the requests for price adjustments swamp the still limited administrative capacities of the agency. Hence, it seemed desirable to announce a policy that would keep requests for relief to a minimum.

movement to a new equilibrium. Stability in the price of wage goods — commodities and services that absorb a large proportion of wage income — is, of course, equally necessary to forestall resulting demands for wage rate advances.

Control of wages and prices of wage goods is central to the strategy of price control in the disequilibrium system. By contrast, control of non-wage civilian goods,* though necessary, is partly a matter of tactics. Higher prices in this area do not, as with increases in the prices of wage goods, lead inevitably to demands for general wage increases. The increased income of sellers does not necessarily trench on the margin of tolerance; depending on the shape of the consumption functions of the affected groups, their increased income may be partially, wholly, or more than offset by the reduction of the spendable funds of others.

In practice, however, the direct controls are not likely to be sufficiently comprehensive or enforceable to keep these higher incomes from being used as an inducement to labor or other resources to enter the non-wage civilian goods industries. Price control is therefore necessary to buttress the direct controls over resource use. Moreover, serious questions of equity and precedent are raised by price movements in this area. High prices and high profits would put wage levels in these industries under pressure; to the extent that the wage controls were circumvented and increases allowed, this would be a precedent for increases elsewhere. The higher profits of producers of non-wage civilian goods would also be a point of reference for producers of wage goods in their demands for price increases. At most, perhaps, the subsidiary or defensive character of price control for non-wage civilian goods

* I have established this awkwardly titled category to avoid using the term "luxuries," which in common usage denotes beer, gasoline for pleasure-driving, and other commodities that enter generally into the worker's budget and which must, accordingly, be considered wage goods. Wartime experience showed that price increases for such items in face of fixed incomes can have the same effect on wage demands as increases in the price of "essentials." The category of non-wage civilian goods exists, in part, because of incomplete mobilization.

suggests only that it need not be as meticulous or as rigorous as for wage goods.*

For war goods, that is, military end products, capital goods, components or materials monopolized or largely monopolized by military employments, price control is, in principle, unnecessary. The monopsony of the procurement authority,† especially when supplemented by power to requisition, is an adequate substitute for price control. Nor need the pricing standards of the procurement authority conform exactly to those of the price control authority. Differentially higher prices for military goods have no obvious repercussion on the price of wage goods; higher profits and a tendency to upgrade wage rates in this area (unlike similar action for non-wage civilian goods) may have beneficial effect on resource use. This expansion of income does, to be sure, cut into the margin of tolerance. But it may be appropriate to use the margin for incentives in this area.

There are limits, of course. At least in the United States, no feature of World War II or more recent mobilization experience has been more striking than the scrutiny which each of the several economic groups brings to bear upon what the others are getting. While differential rates of return which serve a useful purpose can be explained, those that serve no such purpose cannot. Unnecessarily high profits for war goods producers would become the basis of wage claims. And unnecessarily high wages or profits in this area would be cited in support of the demands of producers of wage goods and of wage earners in general.

---

* It was a distinctive feature of price control in the United Kingdom that regulation of non-wage civilian goods was either loose or nonexistent. This accorded more closely with what would be theoretically desirable than practice in the United States or Canada. But it was possible in part because the British controls over resource use, including manpower, were a good deal tighter than in the United States and Canada, in part because more thoroughgoing mobilization of resources had much reduced the importance of this class of goods and in part, it may be assumed, because a sharper stratification of consumption provided more opportunity for discrimination between different classes of goods.

† I assume, of course, unified or reasonably noncompetitive procurement.

In practice, some price control for war goods is also necessary. The three categories of goods and services which I have established are not mutually exclusive, and price control is necessary for those war goods which also enter civilian consumption. The wartime experience also showed that it was convenient to fix prices of commodities like copper and steel, which, although largely monopolized for war purposes, lie several stages removed from finished products. However, this is a procedural detail. Had the Office of Price Administration not controlled the prices of the important industrial materials, the government would have speedily been forced to undertake some sort of bulk procurement, as it did, for example, for rubber. The results in many cases, certainly for such a commodity as lumber, might have been neater.

III

During the course of World War II, price control came increasingly to conform with the principles which, with the aid of hindsight, one can now identify as fundamental in the disequilibrium system. The development was evolutionary in the sense that the final structure was influenced less by an effort to build to an over-all design than by a series of individual decisions each influenced by at least some of the same considerations that would bear on any effort to design a total system.*

* The tendency for isolated decisions to achieve the same result as an effort to follow a general policy is an interesting aspect of government policy-making — perhaps it is what makes government possible. As an example of how individual or microscopic decisions, when fully resolved on their merits, conform to a macroscopic pattern, I think of the problem of price controls on certain kinds of non-wage civilian goods. Nearly all of OPA's critics, at one time or another, attacked these controls — for some reason ceilings on fur coats inspired them to special anger. On several occasions I found myself contending with new colleagues (and once with a new administrator) who were enthusiastic about dropping all price control on fur coats. When they saw that this action would put a premium on high-priced coat manufacture and would draw materials (trim) away from cheaper lines, they soon reversed themselves. In doing so, they more or less unknowingly adopted a position entirely consistent with a broad theoretical pattern for allocating resources and equalizing incentives.

The special importance of wage goods was recognized from the earliest days of price control, although in 1941 and 1942 they shared priority with steel, copper, and other materials in strong wartime demand. During the first months of general price control, special interest legislation made controls over food and clothing the least effective of the regulations. Section 3 of the Emergency Price Control Act made it necessary to exempt whole-sale prices of a considerable range of farm products from regulation because they had not reached the statutory minimum of 110 per cent of parity. In the autumn of 1942, Congress removed the extra 10 per cent handicap, but prices still had to be adjusted to the upward drift of the parity index. Moreover, regulations had to be approved by the Department of Agriculture — a process that almost invariably involved concessions to the inflationary prefer-ences or political hostages of members of that Department. Finally, the Office of Price Administration, though comparatively well organized for control of prices of industrial raw materials, was still ill equipped in 1942 for the immensely more complex task of regulating food and clothing prices. Just as the task was under-taken, the staff that had been built up for controlling food prices was decimated by the demands of the new rationing organization.

By June of 1943, however, control over wage goods had come to conform closely with principle. When the battle smoke of the violent struggles over price control policy in the spring of 1943 blew away, the principle of using subsidies as an alternative to necessary or politically inevitable price increases for wage goods had been established, as had the classification of retail outlets and the establishment of firm dollars and cents prices that the consumer could watch. Although the effort to associate price with quality standards was a disastrous abortion, in the next two years the Bureau of Labor Statistics index of cost of food at retail did not rise at all; it had risen thirty-six points in the two years before.

A case could perhaps be made that non-wage civilian goods

were too rigorously controlled by the OPA. In the earliest stages of planning the General Maximum Price Regulation, it was proposed that these items be exempt from control — the first draft proposal limited the general ceiling to wage goods, or "bread and butter" items, as they were dubbed at the time. In the beginning, such a selective regulation had the support of a substantial majority of the policy-making officials of the agency. After a series of meetings, held daily for nearly a month in the winter of 1942, opinion gradually shifted to favor an inclusive regulation.

It may have remained the sense of those meetings that non-wage civilian goods would be kept under somewhat milder restraint than wage goods. However, in the early months of the GMPR, the proclaimed formula of allowing no price increases had the effect of making all items subject to an equally scrupulous control. There was also some fear that an easygoing policy for non-wage civilian goods would create a legal or moral precedent for similar standards for wage goods. Finally, there was a strong conviction, especially among members of the OPA legal staff, that price stability and inflation were everywhere indivisible. According to this doctrine, a price increase for almost any item could start an "inflationary spiral." While it is doubtful if many of the economists in the agency held this view, it had a powerful influence on price policy.

Quite possibly some form of margin control for non-wage civilian goods would have been sufficient; certainly, a provision for automatic adjustment in case of hardship would have been tolerable. By reducing the strain on the OPA's always over-taxed administrative resources, it might have made the price-fixer's life a little happier and therefore a little longer than it was.

For war goods the wartime experience conformed closely to the requirements of the disequilibrium system. The Emergency Price Control Act itself made no distinction between munitions and civilian goods — when the War and Navy Departments sought, at one stage in deliberations on the bill, to limit the Administrator's authority to price finished armament, they were ordered by President Roosevelt to desist. In the winter and spring of 1942, maximum prices were established by formula for a considerable range of components and subassemblies used in finished armaments. Although, by supplementary regulation, finished armaments, components, and subassemblies were excluded from the General Maximum Price Regulation, plans were made in the summer of 1942 to place formula ceilings on prices of air frames and tanks. A principal objective of these measures was wage control. At the time no effective steps had been taken toward wage stabilization, and it was hoped that these regulations would limit wage increases by making them less painless to arms manufacturers than previously.

Later in the same year the Undersecretaries of War and the Navy sought to have all war goods "without a civilian counterpart" excluded from price control. Partly because of this pressure and partly because wage stabilization had come into being, the Office of Price Administration abandoned the field. By the present standards, this was an appropriate withdrawal; it saved the agency from a complex and unrewarding task and one that, in principle, was unnecessary.*

IV

There remains one further problem, not of policy, but of technique, in the administration of price control under the disequilibrium system. That consists in making an appropriate dis-

---

* The withdrawal was not entirely voluntary, but it was undoubtedly related to a developing appreciation of the system of war mobilization of which price control was a part. For some months prior to the agreement with the War and Navy Departments, I had been growing increasingly uneasy about efforts to control the prices of war goods. I was influenced partly by fear of the blood-spattered criticism we would experience did it ever appear that price controls were delaying the production of arms for men in combat, but also I had begun to doubt that control in this field had any close bearing on the problem of inflation. Leon Henderson, although formally committed to the use of price controls in this area, had, I believe, more than passing sympathy for this view. In any case, the agency did not press its jurisdiction over these goods with anything like its normal vigor.

tinction between imperfect and more or less purely competitive markets and in providing, by way of formal rationing, the necessary reinforcement to price control in the latter markets. This is not a general necessity for all competitive markets, but it is indispensable, particular situations of equilibrium aside, for markets for wage goods. Rationing acquires added significance because two important classes of wage goods, food and clothing, are sold on proximately competitive markets.

In spite of important initial successes, the greatest failure in the operation of the disequilibrium system during World War II was in the association of rationing with price control.

From the earliest days of OPA, or rather of its predecessor agencies, the indispensability of rationing as a supplement to price control was fully recognized by the economists associated with the enterprise — a fact that is hardly surprising in view of the generally unsanguine attitude toward price control as such. The efforts to have administration of price control and rationing associated in the same agency were justified and pressed on economic grounds. For these reasons, a clause was inserted in the original charter of the Office of Price Administration and Civilian Supply (OPACS), giving it authority to make "consumer allocations." * When this authority was later lost to the Supply Priorities and Allocations Board (SPAB), responsibility for rationing rubber tires was obtained from the dying Office of Production Management, because it seemed certain that whatever agency rationed tires would eventually have responsibility for rationing other commodities.

The early rationing programs were ably conceived and executed — a case could be made that the rationing of meats, canned goods, and fuel were among the outstanding administrative achievements of the war. Meat rationing, as I have observed, showed particularly the indispensability of rationing for price

* A euphemism invented at the time because it was feared that the word "rationing" had an unacceptable connotation of scarcity and distress.

control, for it quickly brought order to markets that price control, ex-rationing, had reduced to near chaos. The lesson was fully observed in the OPA.* The markets in which rationing programs were being developed were generally those in which price control required such reinforcement.† This was at least distantly related to a growing appreciation of the different requirements for effective control in different classes of markets.

Yet, as the result of an unhappy combination of bad politics and malignant stupidity, this fine beginning was partially abandoned in favor of helter-skelter distribution at fixed prices. The result was a breakdown of price controls in a number of these markets — the classic breakdown that undergraduates were expected to foretell. The Office of Price Administration was not entirely blameless in this debacle. For a period in 1943 there was a disposition by policy-makers to look upon rationing not as essential for price control but as an unhappy by-product of price regulation. However, the major responsibility for this piece of destruction belonged to the commodity czars who shared responsibility with the OPA for the rationing programs and to the Department of Agriculture. The latter agency in particular was responsible for the doctrine that increased rations would be popular with the American people even though supplies were not available to meet them. The "honoring of ration tickets" had been regarded, by those who designed the system, as the *sine qua non* of suc-

---

* In December of 1942, for example, I suggested to the "Price School" of OPA that we had come to the point where, in some measure, price control "passes out of the hands of the price department and into the hands of the rationing department."

† Perhaps I should make it clear that I do not suggest that support to price control is the only criterion in deciding whether a product should be subject to formal rationing. The product may be of sufficient importance for public health, morale, or efficiency so that the less precise or less equitable controls that would be exercised by sellers in the absence of formal rationing cannot be trusted. The formal rationing of fuel oil during the war had some such rationale. See my paper before the American Economics Association, January 1943, "Price Control: Some Lessons from the First Phase," *American Economic Review Supplement,* March 1943.)

cessful administration. When this principle was breached, the popular basis for rationing disappeared. The consumer was no longer assured of her aliquot share in what was available. The admittedly cumbersome machinery required for effective rationing, when it no longer guaranteed this, became not only burdensome but superfluous. The integrity and even the usefulness of the rationing system having been destroyed, the easy next step was to urge or order the abandonment of all rationing controls. This sealed the fate of price control in the competitive markets and, in some measure, the fate of price control as a whole. The campaign to liquidate price control in the summer of 1946 — a step which, as I shall argue in the next chapter, I believe to have been premature — was enormously strengthened by the manifest breakdown of price regulation in competitive markets, especially in the markets for livestock and meat.*

* For a penetrating and important history of the attack on rationing from within the Executive, see Paul M. O'Leary, *American Political Science Review*, December 1945.

CHAPTER SIX

The employment of the disequilibrium system during a period of crisis leaves a national community with a demanding problem of fiscal management when the crisis is over. People, during the period of emergency, have been given a claim on future civilian goods in return for current effort in the manufacture of military goods. These are liquid claims. After World War II they were held, at the holder's choice, in currency, bank balances, or government bonds, all of which were readily spendable. With the release from controls, the expenditure of these savings is obviously capable of bringing on the inflationary upsurge in prices that the controls had previously restrained.

Such a price increase occurred after the controls were lifted in 1946. This experience, in particular, has led to the suggestion that the practical effect of employing the disequilibrium system in World War II was to postpone to the postwar years the inflation that, given the wartime excess of demand over supply, was ultimately certain to come. It should be noted that even were this true, the use of the disequilibrium system would still be justified: wars cannot be managed with a view to making life simple in the ensuing peace. But the observation is far from defensible. Had prices been allowed to rise without let or hindrance during the war years, had there been the consequent effect on wages and incomes and through these back on prices, and had government expenditures risen as they would necessarily have done in order to procure given requirements at progressively higher prices, the dollar value of the excess of demand would have been progressively increased. Prices would have moved to successively higher positions of equilibrium with at least a strong probability that each movement would have been of greater amplitude than the last. The total of these movements would have borne no necessary relation to the movement resulting from the release of claims accumulated out of an excess of demand at fixed prices, and one cannot suppose that it would have been smaller. In the case of World War II and its aftermath, one can hardly but suppose that it would have been not only greater but vastly greater.

II

Nonetheless, the management of the liquid assets which are the residue of the disequilibrium system presents a problem of undeniable importance. It is possible, as the World War II experience showed, for them to contribute to a painful postwar inflation. This has the same damaging effects as any inflationary movement. Moreover, as I stressed in Chapter IV, the rules of the disequilibrium system require that postwar inflation be prevented. If people are given a promise of future goods or of the security which inheres in liquid assets of assured potential purchasing power in return for present effort, that promise ought to be kept. Inflation represents a partial default on that promise, and apart from the issue of good faith that is involved, the result is to narrow the margin of tolerance for any future employment of the disequilibrium system.

Economists cannot too frequently pause to warn their readers, and also themselves, of the danger in generalizing from any limited experience where the variables are so numerous and their behavior potentially so various as in the *Gestalt* patterns of peace and war. The generalization that wars are followed by deflation and depression, which in the United States was primarily a generalization from the aftermath of the Civil War and World

War I (and which caused men to brace themselves for the same occurrence after World War II) is a warning.

Nevertheless, the experience of World War II does not suggest that the problem of liquidating the disequilibrium system without inflation is insoluble. Our failure to do it after World War II must be attributed primarily, I think, to bad management and bad politics. These, in turn, were not unrelated to our still primitive understanding of the economic system which we had improvised to serve the needs of the war.

The first requirement for a successful liquidation of the disequilibrium system is to view the immediate postwar years as the continuation and counterpart of the war years. In the most general terms, where during the war period the current means of payment are allowed to run ahead of the supply of goods in a context of controls, in the immediate postwar years they must in a similar context be made to run behind. An economy that employs the disequilibrium system in wartime cannot make a direct transition to a peacetime free market. The transition must be by way of what can perhaps best be termed a "counterpart war economy."

There are, in principle and in fact, two ways in which the accumulated liquid assets can be handled so that their effect will be non-inflationary. The first consists in offsetting their use by reducing expenditure elsewhere in the economy. The most important device for accomplishing this is, of course, a budget surplus. A necessary supplement is restraint on new consumer borrowing and, within limits, also on new business investment. In practical terms, a country that has used the disequilibrium system during a period of crisis must expect to keep taxes high and to continue restraints on consumer credit and business investment* for a substantial period after expenditures have fallen.

* The case for restraint here is much less clear than for consumer credit, since in such a period, much of this investment is for conversion or expansion of facilities and thus yields a prompt return in increased output. The problem is to keep total business investment within appropriate limits and, if possible, to win deferment of long-term projects.

For minimizing expenditure from liquid assets and for insuring that such as occurs will be gradual rather than abrupt, the most important factor is the passage of time. It is time, more than anything else, which converts such holdings, in the eyes of their owner, from the status merely of unspent income to that of a reserve fund to be held or drawn on only for some special object or in some emergency. One can say with considerable confidence that, other things equal, the propensity to consume from a stock of savings will be lower the longer that stock has been held.

This means that during the counterpart period, time should be bought by a policy that continues to make spending difficult. Translated into practical measures, this means that the controls, especially the price controls that inhibited spending during the war period and which accounted for the accumulation of the assets, must be continued for a period after the accumulation ceases. The length of the period will obviously be related to the volume of the accumulated claims in relation to the current supply of goods. This introduces, as a consideration, the time during which the supply of civilian goods is being reëstablished — the conversion period — but does not limit the duration of the controls to this period.

III

With the aid of hindsight, it is clear that policies followed after World War II were far from being ideally designed to liquidate the disequilibrium at stable prices. Taxes were reduced promptly and substantially even though there was a sizeable budget surplus in the early postwar years. A very large volume of consumer borrowing for durable goods purchases and of business investment was added to expenditures from current revenues and savings. A government public works program, far outstripping in size anything undertaken during the depression years, was launched almost immediately after the war ended.

Finally, the direct controls over resource use were quickly disestablished. And price control, although it survived for an important twelve months after the Japanese surrender, followed the other controls into discard. At a time when industry had barely completed reconversion to civilian production and when inventories were still seriously depleted,* the accumulated demand was released. The result was a sharper and more persistent upsurge in prices than was experienced at any time during the war. There can surely be little doubt that a more stringent fiscal policy and a more gradual release of controls would have prevented much or all of it.

The argument can be made that by 1946 the price controls, as essentially a wasting asset were no longer useful. There was no other course but a surgical removal. There is no doubt that by 1946 the effectiveness of the controls had been substantially impaired. The proximate cause of this would appear, however, to have been the progressive weakening of the underlying law together with the disintegration of the rationing system already mentioned. There is no clear evidence that time itself, although it had undoubtedly served to educate many in the arts of evasion, was a decisive factor.

A better case can be made for failure of understanding as a cause of the postwar inflation. The implications of the disequilibrium system were not fully appreciated during the war and immediate postwar years. Many of the nation's leaders in economic discussion, drawing on the aftermath of the equilibrium financing of past wars, were calling for measures to forestall a postwar depression. The new social accounts, the pitfalls of which for purposes of prediction economists had not yet fully appreciated, appeared to lend support to this possibility. This was far from

---

* Council of Economic Advisers, *Midyear Economic Report of the President*, July 1951, pp. 246–247. Manufacturers' inventories in relation to sales and those of department stores were both abnormally low in 1946. For the latter, the ratio of inventories to sales was below that of the war years.

being a good environment for measures designed to work off the threat of inflation.

Yet at the time the controls were abandoned in 1946, it was evident to the most detached students of the problem that the inflationary excess of demand had not been worked off and that the result would be a serious rise in prices. The abandonment of controls was forced despite the maladroit and enfeebled efforts of the Administration. The instinct of the Administration was to proceed with the caution that the logic of the disequilibrium system would dictate. In searching for causes something must be attributed to sheer impatience.

As so often happens in American life, the essentially radical course was advocated by conservatives. In this instance the course, designed to weaken capitalism by detracting from the integrity of the promise to the nation's debtors and to force patterns of economic behavior — violent price movements and concomitant industrial strife — that are least easy to defend, was pressed by those who count themselves capitalism's most ardent protectors. Leadership in the campaign was assumed by the National Association of Manufacturers, which also incautiously promised that there would be no inflation.

Without doubt, some who sought the rapid liquidation of controls were motivated by the fear that if they were allowed to last at all, they might last indefinitely. It is difficult to think that this danger was, or is soon likely to be, real. Certainly, such controls do not commend themselves to anyone who ever undertook to administer them. The further argument that controls were inhibiting or would inhibit production was clearly denied by the facts (a) that far more stringent controls had previously been consistent with the largest expansion in product in the nation's history, and (b) that the economy was currently in a state of full or more than full employment. A couple more years of high taxes, of restraint on private borrowing, and of gradually relaxing controls might well have been sufficient for stability and would have been a slight consequence of the largest effort in economic mobilization that any nation had ever attempted. Impatient men insisted that it be otherwise. The dour gods who keep watch on economic policy must muse at the way American capitalism is abused by its most vocal defenders.

CHAPTER SEVEN

The Problem of Limited Mobilization

This essay so far has been concerned with price control under conditions of relatively full mobilization of resources and its aftermath — in a situation, one is permitted to hope, that will remain of only historical interest. The next task is to see whether, and in what measure, the theory and practice appropriate to this extreme or limiting case are relevant to a partial mobilization of economic resources. What is their bearing, in short, on the problems of mobilization policy which we are now (I am writing in the early summer of 1951) facing?

There are important differences between the limited mobilization of resources that the United States and other free members of the United Nations undertook following the outbreak of the Korean war * and a full-scale effort, and these are differences of kind as well as of degree. Because the diversion of resources to military use is limited, the direct control over the use of resources — of plant, materials, and manpower — is also limited. Thus, where full mobilization provides a fairly complete substitute for the allocative function of prices, limited mobilization provides no such substitute. Also, when mobilization is limited, any individual or group can make a strong claim for equitable treatment

---

* The terms "limited" or "partial mobilization," like the terms "middle-aged" and "moderately healthy," do not lend themselves to definition. When I use them, I can only ask that the reader understand that I have in mind the kind and scale of transfer of resources to military use that the United States is now (in the summer of 1951) contemplating.

of his or its real income or property rights, and it cannot be argued that such considerations of equity are among the many civilized values that must necessarily be sacrificed before the *force majeure* of war. There is also room for the expression of some considerable ideological preference in economic policy; that is, if there is a deep and universal aversion to price control, or rationing, or restrictions on house construction, these can be taken into account. When there is full mobilization, the objective of bringing the war to a successful end exercises what is, in effect, a totalitarian veto on individual preferences, and most individuals, recognizing this, bow more or less gracefully to it. No one can suppose that any such surrender of individual preference has been operative in the last twelve months in the United States.

Finally, the sort of limited mobilization on which the United States has recently been engaged has no foreseeable terminal point. The accepted view of the political and military strategy underlying American rearmament is that an effective and modern military force in being is necessary for peace. There may be changes in the rate at which resources are required for building and maintaining such a force; it is presumed that we are currently in a period when the increase in the size of the force and the need to provide modern equipment are creating extraordinary demands. But, in this strategy, no date can be foreseen when the demands will cease. While a poor peace is infinitely to be preferred to any war, it carries with it no similar hope of great change for the better. As a result, elements of national strength, either in resources or much more importantly in organization, cannot be dissipated in the knowledge that the resulting problems can be tackled in a happier day when the all-compelling problems of defense and security have been resolved.

II

Perhaps it is not surprising that, in this general context, the debate over economic policy has been especially sharp — far sharper than it would have been had the mobilization been more nearly complete. The case of Jean Valjean is more difficult for a jury than that of John Dillinger.

In part, this debate has been occasioned by the ubiquitous hope that it may be possible to have mobilization without any of its inconveniences.* Since price control in World War II is remembered by not a few as a notably inconvenient enterprise, it follows for some that the case for avoiding it is especially strong. While business spokesmen and politicians have been most strongly attracted by this syllogism, one senses a certain parallel in the discussion of some professional economists. Instead of examining these controls for their utility or disutility in preventing inflation or facilitating mobilization, they have shown a disposition to dismiss them as uniquely evil in themselves.† It is perhaps well that we occasionally remind ourselves that one reason that the vagaries and discomforts of controls were so evident in the last war was that, during the war itself, inflation was not so evident. The memories of the casualties and discomforts of a successful campaign should not be allowed to disguise the fact that defeat might have been worse.

There have also been substantial objections to the use of price control on rather less ideological grounds, the two most important of which seem to me seriously in error, at least in their emphasis. The first of these objections turns on the damage that results when the allocative function of prices is negated by controls.** That there

---

*Here and in the next few pages I have drawn, with considerable revision and amplification, on a paper I read before the December 1950 meetings of the American Economic Association on "The Strategy of Direct Control in Economic Mobilization," and subsequently published in the February 1951 issue of the *Review of Economics and Statistics*.

† For an extreme but scholarly expression of this viewpoint, see Wytze Gorter and George H. Hildebrand, *American Economic Review*, March 1951.

** For example Professor Bernard F. Haley's comment at the meeting of the American Economic Association in 1949: "The imposition of price ceilings on products employed both in the military and civilian sectors would destroy, partly or wholly, the usefulness of the price system as a mechanism for the allocation of

cannot be control and a normally functioning price system is obvious. I have already indicated that under conditions of partial mobilization we cannot expect that direct controls over resource use will provide a substitute. It does not follow, however, that this is fatal. Resources, after imposition of controls, will continue to flow in the previous channels. If the pre-control allocation was satisfactory, it will remain satisfactory at least for some period. Were this not so, the imposition of price controls, in the absence of companion controls over resource use, would lead immediately to a frightful mix-up in the production and distribution of goods. We should have much too much of some things, much too little of others, and much of everything in the wrong places. This, we now know, does not happen in any dramatic way. Meanwhile, even under partial mobilization, the task of allocating resources to defense uses will have been removed from the price system. And against the danger of reduced allocative efficiency as a result of price control must be set the precisely similar danger resulting from inflation. That danger, it must be kept in mind, can be very great — indeed, inflation places a premium on the withholding of storable resources from all use.

III

The second and much more important shortcoming of the recent discussion has been an undue narrowing of the range of choice in stabilization policy. Specifically, a simple choice has been assumed between a policy of maintaining an equilibrium of demand and supply at stable prices by use of appropriate fiscal and monetary measures — a policy that would employ no price or wage controls — and one of using controls to suppress an inflationary excess of demand. As more commonly and briefly expressed, the choice presented has been between maintaining stabil-

---

that part of these particular resources that would remain for the civilian sector." (See *American Economic Review, Papers and Proceedings*, May 1950, p. 204.)

ity by indirect fiscal and monetary means and suppressed inflation.*

The choice, in fact, is between three possible policies — an equilibrium without controls, a disequilibrium sustained by controls, and an equilibrium of demand and supply supplemented by controls. I shall presently urge that, for purposes of partial mobilization, the latter course is both the safest and the most practical one. This conclusion emerges from an examination of the strengths and shortcomings of the first two.

The case that is made for equilibrium without controls is a comparatively simple one. If, through taxation and restraints on private borrowing, the aggregate of private demand is kept currently equal to the supply of goods and services available for purchase, this will insure price stability. It is also held to be the only valid formula for stability. Price and wage controls will be invoked only if the restraints on private expenditure are insufficient and their effect, accordingly, will be only to suppress what would otherwise be an open inflationary movement. In this argument, typically, the dangers of suppressed inflation are equated with those of open inflation.

It needs to be observed, first of all, that open and suppressed inflation do not represent the same magnitude of danger. To assert that they do is to misapprehend the basic dynamics of inflation in a modern economy. The controls which suppress inflation have the concomitant and all-important effect of also preventing wage and price movements and any tendency for the one to act on the other. If prices and wages are uncontrolled, there is full scope for such interaction, and in the inflationary process this is

---

* See, for example, the policy statement of the Committee for Economic Development, *Paying for Defense* (November 16, 1950). A somewhat similar position — which might well have been modified by later events, for it was written prior to the heavy reverses in Korea in November 1950 — is implied in the interesting and important recommendations of six of my colleagues in the January 1951 issue of the *Harvard Business Review* ("Tax Program for Sustained Mobilization," by J. Keith Butters, William Fellner, John Lintner, Dan Throop Smith, Arthur Smithies, and Stanley S. Surrey).

almost certainly of critical importance. The upward thrust in prices which would result from an excess of demand (say from a budget deficit under conditions of full employment) would be self-equilibrating were there no further interaction of prices and wages. In modern labor and product markets, such a price increase leads inevitably to wage demands. These, if granted, lead, on the one hand, to expanded wage income and to still further pressure on given supplies in the product markets and, on the other hand, via cost increases, to still further price increases. For this process to continue without limit, some continuing supplement to demand is necessary — either a budget deficit, or continued consumer and business dissaving and borrowing. But at full employment the role of such an exogenous supplement to demand is catalytic rather than causal. It is possible for a relatively small government deficit (especially if its existence inhibits policies designed to check the facilitating increase in bank borrowing and therewith the money supply) to catalyze large successive rounds of wage and price increases.

If prices and wages are controlled effectively, then the interaction of wages and prices cannot so act as an accelerant of the inflationary movement. If aggregate demand exceeds supply, the resulting expansion of liquid claims — the suppressed demand — will be equal, or at least related in magnitude, to the initial excess of demand. If the source of the excess of demand is a budget deficit, the suppressed demand will be greater or less as the deficit is larger or smaller. In all cases the ultimate effect will be much more circumscribed than had a wage-price spiral proceeded without hindrance.*

---

* Economists, not without reason, have long been suspicious of explanations of economic phenomena which turn on the sequential interaction of one variable on another. It is fatally easy to show, for example, how a reduction in farm prices causes a reduction in farmer's expenditures, in the income of non-farm enterprises, in the demand of wage earners of the latter for farm products, and on to a further decline in farm prices. Such verbal constructions have a great fascina-

Herein lies the difference between open and suppressed inflation. The first has a powerful dynamic of its own; the rate and
extent of the movement need bear no relation to the initiating
excess of demand. The effects of suppressed inflation are limited
to the effects of the current excess of demand. In lay terms, open
inflation can run away; suppressed inflation cannot.

To return now to equilibrium management of a partially
mobilized economy. The interaction of prices on wages and wages
on prices just sketched offers a major threat to such a policy. In
the context of partial mobilization, a maximum of production will
almost certainly be sought from the economy; as a result, demand,
even though not in excess of supply, will be sufficient to keep
resources fully employed. This means that in any given product
market and in its counterpart market for labor or other factors,
demand will be inelastic. Put in other terms, if demand is pressing
on the capacity of the labor force, wages can be advanced without
any serious fear, in the given case, of unemployment; if product
demand is strong enough so that labor and other resources are
being actively sought after by entrepreneurs, then product prices
can be advanced without fear of loss of sales volume. It is supply
availability at the going price, not the price, that sets the limit on
sales. Under these circumstances there is no real conflict of interest between management and unions.* The interests of both can
be readily reconciled by wage and price increases.

The possibility of such an amicable, if inflationary, resolution

---

tion to newcomers to economics, and the total speciousness of the conclusions that
are usually reached has led, I think, to a kind of methodological ban on all such
reasoning. The wage-price spiral, a phenomenon which anyone with eyes must
conclude is wholly real, has fallen partly under this ban.

  * For a more detailed analysis of this tendency toward *de facto* coalition between management and labor under inflationary conditions in modern labor and
product markets, I venture to refer to my *American Capitalism: The Concept of
Countervailing Power* (Boston: Houghton Mifflin, 1952).

of management-labor conflict in the absence of controls is much greater now than it was during World War II. Then management was fresh from the bitter organization battles of the later thirties. These had reinforced the ancient suspicion of employers that organized labor is usually wrong, and its demands generally inimical to the welfare both of business and society. This attitude was not favorable to automatic or easy concessions to labor even when there was no short-run justification for resistance. Equally important, the end of the war was foreseen. Then, it was agreed, there would be a day of reckoning for the industry or firm which had allowed wage increases and adjustments to raise its breakeven point to what might prove to be a dangerous level.

None of these restraints now operate. In contrast with the bitterness and bellicosity of the industrial relations of a mere ten years ago, the modern accent is on mellowness in collective bargaining. The employer who cannot get along with his union has become hopelessly *déclassé*. He is tactfully but firmly excluded from the list of after-luncheon speakers; he must himself listen to the modern hero, the man who has negotiated twenty contracts but never had a strike. Now there is no vision (or specter) of an early V-J Day which will leave wages and breakeven points high in the face of dwindling volume. On the contrary, a business community which bases its economic judgments of the future on what it has most recently experienced will assume that the present period of crisis will end, to the extent that an end is foreseen at all, as did the last, in inflation. It will not be supposed that wage levels that are established in the interim will prove embarrassing.

Under all these circumstances, it will be the general policy of management to accede promptly and fully to labor demands and to recoup on prices. No other course is plausible or possibly even rational. The President of the United States Steel Corporation showed the shape of things now and to come when, in November 1950, he volunteered a wage increase to the union as long as it conformed to the general pattern of the fifth round. He went on to assert, in full harmony with the above analysis, that the "half cent" inflation which would result was a small price to pay for "uninterrupted and expanded" production.

In principle, if demand is rigorously restrained, any upward movement in wages and prices will at some point have to come to a stop. Price increases, if made, will at some point result in reduced sales — elasticity will have reappeared in product demand schedules. And wage increases for this reason will be resisted or, if offered, will result in reduced employment.

There is no need to stress the rigor of the measures to control demand that such a policy requires. In the context, moreover, one normal instrument of government fiscal policy, the reduction of total government expenditures, is unavailable. What is to be spent for arms, the controlling component in the total, must be taken as given; it is not susceptible to reduction in the interests of stability.

However, the possibility of a rigorous policy may be conceded; indeed it will be evident in a moment that I feel such a policy to be necessary. But such an equilibrium, without controls, also assumes that the community is willing to make some sacrifice of production and tolerate the continuation of normal-management labor disputes and consequent occasional work stoppages, in the interest of stability. An approximate balance of supply and aggregate demand at full employment levels is not, of itself, an assurance of stability. If such restraints are to be effective, they must reduce demand somewhat below full employment levels — they must create enough slack in product and factor markets so that demand schedules are no longer inelastic. Stability must be won at some sacrifice in employment and production.

This is not a sacrifice that is likely to be made when resources are being diverted to military use and when the economy is under pressure to produce enough for both soldiers and civilians. The remaining choice is between controls in some form and the inflation implicit in successive rounds of wage and price increases.

Thus, if limited mobilization makes imperative the full (and peaceful) use of resources, there is a case for the use of wage and price controls. However, the case does not extend to justify the full deployment of the disequilibrium system. On the contrary, there are strong reasons for believing that wage and price controls should perform their important and perhaps indispensable function with the closest practical approach to a demand-supply equilibrium.

The case for the disequilibrium system under conditions of full mobilization rests strongly on the need to use the incentive value of money claims to be held for later expenditure or security at a time when the resources available for the production of civilian goods are at a minimum. When resources are only partially mobilized, the need for this expedient disappears. There are currently produced goods and services of nearly all kinds for which workers can work. There is no prima facie need for supplementing these with a claim on future production.

There are also positive disadvantages from use of the disequilibrium system in a context of partial resource mobilization. Under such circumstances, the direct controls over resource use are not likely to be comprehensive or especially strong. This means that excess demand can readily find channels in which it can be effective, and it will take resources with it. The alternative to spending is not, as with full mobilization, involuntary (though not unwelcome) saving. In an economy that is fully mobilized, the race tracks are closed. In a partially mobilized economy, excess demand can go to the tracks and take with it the bearer and additional pari-mutuel operators, bookmakers. handicappers, tipsters, touts, hostlers, jockeys, Pinkertons, and other more or less useful labor. Much has been said, and properly, of the inefficiencies which are the by-product of suppressed demand. It has not been so clearly recognized, however, that this is a function of the alternative outlets for expenditure and that these diminish progressively, the more complete the control over resource use. What is a problem of first-rate importance in a partially controlled economy becomes much less significant in a fully controlled one.*

Last, and most important, the kind of limited mobilization which we are now undertaking has no terminal date. Thus no promise can be made of a time when money claims can be covered by goods. This means that the margin of tolerance is relatively narrow, and it has already been made clear that it is also a wasting asset. To use the disequilibrium system under present circumstances would mean the progressive narrowing of the margin of tolerance and in advance of what might be a day of greater need.

Thus, to summarize, wage and price controls are probably necessary in a state of limited mobilization. They ought, however, to be employed under conditions of an approximate equilibrium of demand and supply. They are an adjunct of the monetary and fiscal measures which maintain this equilibrium. Their specific and rather limited function is to prevent the interaction of prices and wages where the imperative of maximized production requires full use of current resources, particularly of labor.

---

* Its significance does not disappear. In the United Kingdom, during World War II and in spite of comprehensive and rigorous controls, there was continuing complaint about the escape of resources into low-grade use. The most discussed manifestation of this was the "spivs," the men who made a wartime profession out of catering to the less disciplined tastes of Englishmen. However, the problem of inefficiency associated with an excess of demand became an acute issue in the United Kingdom only in postwar years as the controls over resource use were somewhat relaxed as were also the patriotic compulsions of the war period.

CHAPTER EIGHT

Price Control and Limited Mobilization

As the final task of this book, an outline can now be given of the central strategy of price control — or rather of price and wage control — under conditions of limited mobilization.

The function of such controls, it follows from the discussion of the last chapter, is to prevent the interaction of prices and wages when the economy is functioning at the current capacity of its labor force. Such reciprocal movements of prices and wages characterize only a part of the economy. They are commonplace where strong unions bargain with corporations that have a strong position in product markets. They do not occur at all in agriculture where there are no unions and where no individual producer of staples has any discretionary power over his prices. Agricultural prices, in the short-run with which I am here dealing, make no response to changes in cost rates. Thus, very roughly, the problem of wage-price interaction is a problem of that part of the economy where there is market imperfection, oligopoly in particular, and it ceases to be a problem in those industries that approach pure competition in their product markets.

If the substantive contribution of the controls is to prevent the wage-price interaction, it follows that the controls have an important service to render only in imperfect markets. These are also the markets, as the discussion of Chapters II and III has made clear, which are most amenable to control. This is not an accident.

The same market imperfections which facilitate price control provide the setting for the interaction of wages and prices which the controls prevent.

In an ideal model of inflation control when the requisite restraint is being kept on demand, price controls would be confined to imperfect markets where prices are administratively determined. Wage controls would be confined to those wages that are set by collective bargaining with effective unions. The wage and price controls so established would apply roughly to the same part of the economy, for in general, in the United States, there are strong unions where there are strong firms in product markets. However, in both principle and practice, the control should also apply to the administrative discretion of those unions — in coalmining and clothing manufacture, for example — where there is an approximation to pure competition in the product markets. In product markets which approach pure competition and in unorganized labor markets, stability in prices or rates would be the counterpart of the control of demand.

The foregoing means, in practical terms, that the steel, automotive, electrical, chemical, and like industries would be under price control, as would the wages of the unions with which those industries deal. In this part of the economy, firms have undoubted discretion to move their prices. And such movements are made in response to the cost-shoving * effect of wage increases. On the other hand, prices in primary agricultural markets, clothing prices, and perhaps also margins for the generality of retail trade would be left uncontrolled. Since they are demand determined, and *if* demand is limited to available supply and is expected so to remain, they should show no tendency in the aggregate to rise. In this part of the economy, there is no built-in dynamic of price-cost movement even at full-employment demand.

---

* As distinct from "demand-pulling" effects which rule in competitive markets. This is the terminology employed by Professor Albert G. Hart in his admirable book, *Defense without Inflation* (New York: Twentieth Century Fund, 1951).

II

Within the past year, 1951, there has been an interesting tendency for price and wage control to approximate in practice, although not by design, the formula just suggested. Wage stabilization is largely, although by no means exclusively, effective in areas where collective bargaining is the rule. The unorganized employees of farmers and other small firms enjoy either a *de facto* or *de jure* exemption from wage stabilization. Moreover, the General Manufacturers Regulation,* covering the generality of processing and fabricating industries, covers very roughly the area of administrative pricing in product markets. At the other extreme are agricultural markets where, as the result of politics abetted by administrative difficulty, there has been little effective control other than that exercised by demand.

However, the distinctions here being made are unlikely ever to be employed deliberately for deciding where there should be control and where there should be none. Price control in the United States has come to be regarded as something which must have general application — as a cross which should burden everyone or no one. Apart from the very difficult distinctions that would be involved in limiting it to imperfect markets and administered prices, the political implications of *seeming* to leave such important cost-of-living items as food and clothing uncontrolled would probably be fatal to wage stabilization. Union leadership in the United States undoubtedly has a high level of economic literacy, but it would be a taxing job to explain to labor why wages must be fixed while agricultural prices are susceptible to control by indirect means. Such a policy would also require a high degree of confidence on the part of all in the capacity of the government to employ the monetary and fiscal restraints to the full extent necessary for equilibrium at going prices.

* Office of Price Stabilization, Ceiling Price Regulation 22.

There is the further difficulty that, even within a general framework of demand and supply, developments in particular competitive markets can be such as to have disequilibrating effects of a serious nature. In the past year the livestock industry, particularly beef production, has presented a problem of this character. The income elasticity of meat demand, especially that for beef, is very high. A substantial part of our agricultural land and capital resources are readily convertible to beef production. This has relatively flexible labor requirements at a time when uncertainties in the farm labor market make this a desideratum, and beef and meat production generally are heavy claimants on feed supplies. Under these circumstances, high meat prices — and especially high beef prices — are to be expected in the absence of controls with attendant effects on wage stability. And a considerable if not a major part of the responding increase in production will draw resources from other agricultural production with serious potential effects on food and fiber supply in general. Such special equilibrium situations may have to be dealt with specifically; it cannot be assumed that indirect measures will suffice.

III

Under all these circumstances, it must be expected that price control in the United States will mean price control across-the-board — or across-the-board with only such exceptions as an agrarian-minded Congress makes for reasons of votes of farmers or other special interest groups, rather than for reasons of economics. However, the difference in the role of price control in different sectors of the economy loses little if any importance for this reason. Even though prices of competitively produced products are fixed, the ceilings ought not to be regarded as a pivot of the stabilization effort. The objective in such markets, particular problems of disequilibrium apart,* is to keep the ceilings from

---

* And in these cases the price control, it seems scarcely necessary to repeat, must be paced by steps to control demand for the particular product or products.

being under pressure. The test of a successful inflation control policy in competitive markets is that prices are at least occasionally below ceiling levels. The appearance of shortages on any important scale should be a major warning. The imperfect or administered markets require no similar policy and yield no such warnings. In the over-all strategy of inflation control, it is the competitive markets which tell whether demand is being kept in balance with supply — whether, in the aggregate, the kind of stabilization appropriate to partial mobilization is being achieved or is not.

IV

In these chapters, I have been dealing with the economic principles and problems that underlie or result from price control. While they have not been entirely excluded, I have had comparatively little to say about the administration of controls or of the almost uniquely ardent political atmosphere in which the price-fixer works. Anyone who has been associated with this enterprise will assert that of the various facets of the price-fixer's task — economic, administrative, and political — I have dealt with the easiest.

It is the administration of price control and its obscene politics, far more than its economics, which lead me to wish for a peaceful world in which price regulation refers once again only to a limited war between private utilities and the government. However, if we are fated to live in a world of tension, a prospect I have myself not yet quite accepted, then inflation and the means of preventing it are as likely to be part of our destiny as the draft. Price control, although still far from being universally so accepted, does, I am persuaded, have an important and perhaps an indispensable place in the pharmacopoeia of inflation remedies. In any

---

No doubt, there will still be hapless administrators who will try to fix prices and, in face of a substantial disequilibrium, try to avoid rationing in such markets. Both they and the public will regret the outcome of an experiment the failure of which can be foretold more readily than most happenings in economics.

case, we are using it, and those who doubt that it is necessary or wise should remember that in the incommensurable task of governing this Republic, we often do in practice what we only later find to be justified in principle. If this be so in the case of price control, we shall need in days to come to bring to the analysis of the controlled market some of the energies that have heretofore and are now being invested in the free one. Even though we do not like what we are doing, we should understand what we are about.

INDEX

INDEX

''/S